THERE IS NO BEAR.

THERE IS NO BEAR.

Just Breathe.

Preparing for the Inevitable
Conflicts of Life with Strangers,
the Church, Family, Friends, and God.

Kristy Easley

Xulon Elite

Xulon Press Elite
555 Winderley Pl, Suite 225
Maitland, FL 32751
407.339.4217
www.xulonpress.com

© 2024 by Kristy Easley

All rights reserved solely by the author. The author guarantees all contents are original and do not infringe upon the legal rights of any other person or work. No part of this book may be reproduced in any form without the permission of the author.

Due to the changing nature of the Internet, if there are any web addresses, links, or URLs included in this manuscript, these may have been altered and may no longer be accessible. The views and opinions shared in this book belong solely to the author and do not necessarily reflect those of the publisher. The publisher therefore disclaims responsibility for the views or opinions expressed within the work.

Unless otherwise indicated, Scripture quotations taken from the Holy Bible, New International Version (NIV). Copyright © 1973, 1978, 1984, 2011 by Biblica, Inc.™. Used by permission. All rights reserved.

Scripture quotations taken from The Message (MSG). Copyright © 1993, 1994, 1995, 1996, 2000, 2001, 2002. Used by permission of NavPress Publishing Group. Used by permission. All rights reserved.

Scripture quotations taken from the New Revised Standard Version (NRSV). Copyright © 1989 the Division of Christian Education of the National Council of the Churches of Christ in the United States of America.

Scripture quotations taken from the New King James Version (NKJV). Copyright © 1982 by Thomas Nelson, Inc. Used by permission. All rights reserved.

Scripture quotations taken from the English Standard Version (ESV). Copyright © 2001 by Crossway, a publishing ministry of Good News Publishers. Used by permission. All rights reserved.

Paperback ISBN-13: 978-1-66289-834-1
Ebook ISBN-13: 978-1-66289-835-8

To my love and greatest champion, David, thank you for your unwavering faith and belief in me and for loving me so well. I look forward to many more adventures together.

Table Of Contents

Acknowledgments ix
Preface xi

Section I – Where to Begin?

    Introduction – Just Breathe xiii
    Chapter 1 – What Is It? 1

Section II – Preparation

    Chapter 2 – The Main Character. 13
    Chapter 3 – Emotional Excavation 27
    Chapter 4 – Name Them and Claim Them 41
    Chapter 5 – Building Fences 59
    Chapter 6 – The Line That Will Not Be Crossed 69

Section III – The Fights That Find Us

    Chapter 7 – The Reactions We Do Not Choose:
                    The FFFF Responses 81
    Chapter 8 – Flipping Your Lid 91
    Chapter 9 – Flipped Lid 105

Section IV – Pick Your Battles

    Chapter 10 – What is Worthy of the Fight? 117
    Chapter 11 – Church Conflict: Not Mine to Do 137
    Chapter 12 – Church Conflict: Taking a Stand. 151
    Chapter 13 – Church Conflict: Lessons Learned 169

Section V – Conflict with the Ones We Know Well

    Chapter 14 – Conflict with Family, Friends and God 179

Conclusion 199

Acknowledgements

TO ALL OF my friends and family members who have answered questions, sat through hard conversations, and shared their views on conflict with me, thank you.

To the few dear people who read some very rough first drafts and gave me valuable feedback, thank you! I am forever grateful.

Two women helped formulate reflection and discussion questions found at the end of each chapter:

- My daughter, friend, and wise counsel, Rachel Easley Yarborough (MA, LPC), despite her busy schedule as a sought-after therapist in the Austin area, managing two other businesses, and raising my three precious grandchildren, made time in her beautiful and crazy life to read many chapters of this book. Rachel, your time and effort in reading chapters and composing questions are deeply appreciated. Your input was invaluable to me.
- Trisha Taylor (MA, LPC) is my long-time friend and favorite conversationalist. She has been a pastoral counselor for more than thirty years, an ordained minister, and co-founder of The Leader's Journey: Coaching for Wholehearted Leadership. Trisha, thank you so much for your generous contributions to this book. Your encouragement has kept me going and moving forward. I look forward to many more conversations, walks, and learning to "just breathe" together.

To my husband, David Easley (MD), I am deeply grateful for your role as my scientific adviser. Your meticulous reading of every word of this book, from the Preface to the Conclusion, and your invaluable input, suggestions, and corrections have been instrumental in shaping this work. Thank you for your unwavering support and dedication.

Preface

BY THE BEGINNING of 2022, I had grown weary of loud and heated discussions about differing opinions. I was tired of all the anger and fighting that seemed to be raging around me 24/7 via the news cycles, social media, and anywhere else two or more were gathered. I naively thought America would calm down after the presidential election of 2020. It didn't. National anxiety only ramped up as we faced the Coronavirus. I naively believed that a global pandemic would unite the country like a Coca-Cola commercial at Christmas, and we would all sing "in perfect harmony." We did not. The nationwide discord was loud and chaotic, like a middle school jazz concert without an end. Somewhere along the way, people had forgotten how to be civil and kind. The name of our country, The United States of America, was false. The unification of America was a distant dream.

Few topics were free from controversy. There was no safe haven void of uncomfortable conversations. Even churches disagreed on everything from politics to mask mandates. It became apparent that conflict was a mainstay of the American culture, and I had better get used to it. I needed to discover a different way of participating in the inevitable conflicts that confronted me daily. I desired to learn to communicate my thoughts and opinions with others better. I didn't want to run away from uncomfortable conversations, but I didn't want to damage relationships. I wanted to engage with people more effectively, but I needed to gain the skills and knowledge to do that.

I began reading books, listening to podcasts, observing conversations, listening intently to differing viewpoints, and understanding my patterns and behaviors surrounding conflict. I studied and sought out experts in psychology and social reform. I also dove deep into the Bible, listened to sermons, and read books by respected Christian authors. How did Jesus deal with conflict? What could I learn by reading scripture through the lens of the opposition Jesus faced? How did he handle controversy when it confronted him? What clarity could I gain by studying Jesus through the lens of conflict? I know Jesus pushed back against religious leaders. What made his fight so effective? I looked at disputes recorded in scripture. What could I gain by learning more about them? The result of a two-year journey to find a better way culminated in the writing of this book.

There are a few things from my background that influenced this book and will be helpful for the reader to know. My Theatre Arts and English degrees shaped how I interpreted and presented the idea of conflict. A literary diagram of the Climatic Plot Structure was chosen to show the different stages of conflict. My experience dissecting characters and plots was helpful in understanding and sharing real-life situations. My extended study of the Enneagram Personality Profiling System was also instrumental in understanding and explaining how conflict can be expressed and viewed so differently from person to person.

I did not write this book because I am qualified or an expert on the topic of conflict. I chose this topic because it is an area in which I needed more knowledge. I have learned so much in the process of writing this book. It is my hope you can find some solutions to your own areas of conflict within these pages.

Introduction

Just Breathe

> "There is nothing nominal or lukewarm or indifferent about standing in this hurricane of questions every day and staring each one down until you've mustered all the bravery and fortitude and trust it takes to whisper just one of them out loud."[1] Rachel Held Evans

IN THE BACKYARD of my childhood home was an old, rusted swing set. The seesaw and swings had been removed at some point, leaving only a naked stand. It was more of a swing set skeleton. Its weathered bones created a triangular fixture in our backyard like two metal A's suspended in the air by a single pipe. The frame's original color was a mystery, as the paint had chipped off long ago. However, I remember the green wooden swing hung from the pipes at some point in my childhood, a porch swing with gray-silver chains. It was a swing a young girl could lay on and methodically swing back and forth, back and forth, back and forth. Metal against metal creaking a comforting rhythmic message of "just breathe, just breathe, just breathe." The trees above me danced in front of a sky background. The clouds added to the dizzying effect. The windier the day, the better. The tree limbs moved like a wild, impromptu modern dance, seemingly chaotic yet divinely orchestrated. How is it that stiff branches can appear so fluid? My pre-adolescent

---

[1] Rachel Held Evans, *Searching for Sunday: Loving, Leaving, and Finding the Church*

self often escaped to the soothing motion of the swing. Problems were solved, dreams were dreamed, and imagination was ignited with each sway. In retrospect, the gentle movement of the swing met some innate need of mine, a stimming of sorts, centering myself, self-regulating. I coveted the solitude of those moments and wanted more of them. It's not that I didn't like people. I did…very much. But I also wanted to be alone…very much.

My superpower growing up was the power of invisibility. I could make myself small and quiet and blend into the background. When you are a child, if you're quiet long enough, people tend to forget you are in the room. You become an audience of one watching real life without any affectation; no one performs because they don't know there's an audience. I'd often watch my lovely, crazy aunts cook in the kitchen. They were wildly entertaining, much better than any television show. Reality shows weren't even a thing at the time. I would listen in on adult conversations, not in a creepy, invasive way. I was just curious, or maybe more intrigued than curious. I found people fascinating. Why did they say the things they did, I wondered? Why did they laugh at his jokes but giggle more at hers? Why did they lean in when certain people spoke but lean away from others?

One of my favorite real-life reality shows happened almost every weekend. Most Friday nights, my parents would have family friends over to our house, or we would go to theirs. The adults would play 42, a domino version of Hearts or Spades. My parents and their friends would play until well after midnight. I find it humorous now that they drank coffee when they played. Alcohol was "forbidden" as we were Southern Baptists, but why drink coffee late at night? I guess it was to keep them awake after a long work week, but the smell of coffee still sends me back to those pleasant memories. The host for the evening always ushered the kids to a back bedroom equipped with food and a TV. Late in the night, we watched an inappropriate show called "Project Terror." I wonder if the adults knew what we were watching or that two teenagers often made out during commercial breaks. Needless to say, both forms of entertainment were rather repulsive to a ten-year-old girl. Usually, I would leave the man-eating zombies and the kissy face and slither down the hall to be within earshot of the adults. I'd slide onto the floor hidden within my invisible cloak and listen to the beautiful sounds of old friends enjoying easy camaraderie over coffee and dominoes. Those sights, sounds, and smells were soothing and stabilizing. I loved how there would be minutes of silence leading up to loud sounds of victory or defeat as someone plopped down the last domino all good-natured and in great fun. My childhood was secure, full of these soothing moments, "just breathe, just breathe, just breathe".

I remember another game of dominoes, the tone very different. Each summer, my family attended a family reunion. Inevitably, we would go to the same lakeside retreat. Summer activities in Texas are best done near water. The irony was that few people went outside the metal building where we gathered, the air-conditioner struggling to combat the heat and humidity. We would arrive early in the day with shirts already sticking to our backs. Summers in Texas are not for the weak or faint of heart. Every summer, food would be abundant. The metal building would reverberate with noise. Every twelve months, the same people greeted one another with hugs and loud pronouncements of "it's been too long." Each year, the deviled eggs would set out on the folding tables for far too long, and each year two brothers would inevitably get into a massive argument over something. Some would call it an argument, others a heated discussion. I deemed it an out-and-out fight. One memorable year, the brothers' battle was over a game of 42. One brother accused the other brother of cheating. It was loud, volatile, and personal. The other players at the table kept their eyes downcast. They did not engage in the controversy and quietly put the dominos away for the rest of the weekend.

In my little girl world, this argument was monumental. We did not argue in my house. My parents' disagreements were behind closed doors or, at best, quiet and controlled. The raised voices and gestures of the two men were frightening and unfamiliar. I did not like it. Does anyone really like a fight? Well, yes. My uncles must have because they repeated this behavior at most family gatherings. Their sisters also must have enjoyed it as they often covered their giggles with their hands. Others ignored the whole scene, pretending it never happened, even though it happened yearly. I was fascinated by these scenes but also repulsed by them. What made grown men act this way around a game table? Why did people respond the way they did? Did anyone else notice these as awkward and unwanted exchanges?

The green wooden swing is no longer in the backyard of my childhood home. It is long gone. Not only have I lost my swing, but I've also lost the power of invisibility. I have tried to tap into that superpower as an adult. It doesn't work anymore. People don't think you're invisible when you don't engage in conversations. They just think you're weird or aloof. I like people. I really do. I like chatting with store owners and random people in the grocery store. I enjoy asking strangers questions about themselves. Relationships in their infancy are safe. Keep the conversations light and airy–just lots of friendly icebreaker questions. It's the sticky middle part of relationships I dread.

Inevitably, every human connection will have disagreements, heated discussions, arguments, or fights. I hate conflict. I don't want to deal with it ever. I am an adult, however, and apparently, conflict is a part of adulting. As my kids say, "adulting is hard." When did adult become a verb?

The ironic and challenging truth for those of us who would choose to avoid all conflict is that avoidance of conflict can sometimes perpetuate conflict. Avoiding issues means there are never resolutions! It is tricky and exhausting. I am learning my childhood way of dealing with the world is no longer serving me. My desire for harmony with the people around me contradicts my need for deep human connection. Good and healthy relationships require good and healthy discussions, which sometimes result in conflictual opinions.

Just Breathe

My personality leans in the direction of being more passive than aggressive. I want things to just resolve on their own and get better over time. There is the pressure I feel as a Christian woman to turn the other cheek, be gracious at all times, and do everything I can to smooth things over. But, if I'm honest, overly passive reactions haven't been serving me or others well. While being passive may look good at first, if I'm letting the tension in a situation build and intensify, I run the risk of getting so worn out from the hard dynamics at play that I start slipping back into immature reactions and un-healthy patterns.[2]

I knew I wasn't handling conflict well when I started avoiding people in 2021. The loud and volatile political landscape in America and the global pandemic had left me disillusioned about people in general. My peaceful mantra of "just breathe" was replaced by the haunting sound of George Floyd's painful cry "I can't breathe. I can't breathe" as police knelt on his chest.[3]

Living on a deserted island became my secret fantasy. Now that I think about it, a castle surrounded by a massive moat with a drawbridge would be better than an island. My imaginary moat would be full of hungry alligators and deadly sharks. I'm unsure if alligators and sharks can live in the same water, but this is my fantasy, so I can make it what I want. In the castle, I would sit in a very tall tower so that I could see anyone approaching. If anyone wanted to come inside my castle and talk to me, they would shout their intentions for their visit from the other side of the moat. They would then sign a waiver stating they would not bring up any topic that might ignite any controversy. If

---

[2] Lysa Terkeurtst, *Good Boundaries and Goodbyes: Loving Others without Losing the Best of Who You Are* (Nashville Tennessee, Nelson Books, 2022) pp. 91-92.

[3] https://www.theguardian.com/us-news/2020/jul/08/george-floyd-police-killing-transcript-i-cant-breathe

any unwelcome topic were brought up, the person would be expelled immediately from the castle.

I knew I was really in trouble when I desired peace more than relationships. By the turn of 2022, I had walled myself off from friends and family, creating a safety buffer to avoid confrontation because loud confrontations were happening everywhere. However, my walls also created a barrier to relationships. I was at a crossroads. Conflicting opinions were unavoidable, if I were to function in this world. I had a choice. Build a castle or deal with conflict better.

My family faced a tough year in 2022. My third grandchild was born on Feb 3, 2022. She was admitted to the hospital a week after her birth and didn't come home for 98 long days. Her health challenges opened my eyes to the need for a village to come alongside me and hold me up when I was too weak to hold myself. The same year, my parents passed away after long, hard, and lingering ends. I experienced the beauty of enduring relationships as I saw friends and their church love them all the way home.

The culmination of all that happened in 2022 changed my trajectory. I moved from a self-proclaimed hermit to a tentative social human. I realized I was not meant to live in a castle or a deserted island. I needed my people and realized how much I had missed them. I saw the church do what it is meant to do: love and care for its flock. I returned to my people and church with a tender, worn, and tired heart. My friends and family had never left me, even when I was oddly absent from their lives. I again engaged in all the wonderful messiness that comes with people.

I treasure my old, tried, and true friendships. We have weathered storms and seen the worst and the best of each other, like battered ships that have arrived at a safe harbor of intimacy. I'm talking about friends who have walked through the most challenging parts of life with me and I with them. The people I once had on speed dial now reside on my favorites list. These people know that part of me I shamefully hide from others and sometimes even myself, but they choose to love me anyway. This kind of intimacy doesn't happen without vulnerability, and vulnerability doesn't happen without risk. You can be sure that these relationships have had their share of disagreements, debates, hurt feelings, eye-rolling in front of and behind backs, misunderstandings, and passive silence. Still, somehow, we have always returned to each other. These relationships don't just take time. They require deep, challenging conversations and a fair share of conflict.

> In a world where perfectionism, pleasing, and proving are used as armor to protect our egos and our feelings, it takes a lot of courage to show up and be all in when we can't control the outcome. It also takes discipline and self-awareness to understand what to share and with whom. Vulnerability is not oversharing, it's sharing with people who have earned the right to hear our stories and our experiences.[4]

Literature, history, excellent teachers, and life experiences have challenged my idea of conflict, helping me to understand how constructive change can come only through challenging discourse. Conflict is necessary for positive change and growth. I am forever grateful to my 5th-grade teacher, Mrs. Wilkerson, who assigned me Rosa Parks as the topic for an oral report. My study of Miss Parks taught me the importance of taking a stand, or in her case, a seat, to fight for necessary change. Through the years, I have cheered for those who advocate for change and remain true to their ideals at significant personal risk.

I don't want to be known as someone who runs away from a challenge. I don't want it written on my tombstone: "She lived an un-challenging life well in a mediocre fashion." I have flashbacks of my past and see how I dodged conflicts like they were lethal bullets—times when I could have been an advocate for needed change and was not. I cringe at the rare battles I rushed into clumsily, only to feel like an utter

---

[4] Brene Brown, *Atlas of the Heart: Mapping Meaningful Connection and the Language of Human Experience* (New York, Random House) p. 14.

fool–my lack of skills falling short of the intended goal. Sometimes, I imagine re-living my life and getting it right this time…a second chance…a do-over. But alas, it is not a possibility. I hope there is a way to till and tend a new garden equipped with new tools and good soil, dig up the hard lessons, failings, and successes, and examine whether they are unwanted weeds or viable plants. I know I have more questions than answers, but in the words of Maya Angelou, "When you know better, you do better." I want to do better. I suspect if you're reading this, you do, too.

Chapter 1

What is it?

That's the main difference between high conflict and good conflict. It's not usually a function of the subject of the conflict. Nor is it about the yelling. It's about the stagnation. In healthy conflict, there is movement. Questions get asked. Curiosity exists. There can be yelling too. But healthy conflict leads somewhere.[5]

DEFINING CONFLICT CAN be tricky. We each have a unique radar for recognizing conflict. Experiences, tolerance levels, and personalities play a part in understanding and perceiving life's oppositions. I recently had lunch with a friend and shared that I was writing a book on conflict. She replied, "Oh, I hate conflict. I avoid it at all cost." Minutes later, she made a loud statement in a crowded restaurant regarding gun control that had me looking around for angry Texans locked and loaded, ready for a shootout. I mean, come on! Did she really hate conflict, or did she want to instigate it? She and I obviously perceived conflict differently. Anything said definitively can be ammunition for a fight...in my opinion.

My husband, David, was on the debate team in high school. He was a champion debater, complete with horn-rimmed glasses and braces. Bless his heart. He was a late bloomer. I assure you he grew into a very

---

[5] Amanda Ripley, *High Conflict: Why We Get Trapped and How We Get Out of It* (New York, New York, Simon & Schuster, 2021) 27.

handsome and successful man. His years on the debate team left him well-trained to see two sides to everything. I mean everything. My son-in-law, Chase, often seeks him out for advice but will come to me for clarification. David views the question from every angle imaginable, sharing a wide berth of information and opinions. Most of the time, you need help to guess what he thinks is the best option. After conferring with my husband, Chase usually becomes more unsure of what David thinks is the best decision, but he always leaves well-informed! Friends call David the devil's advocate. A devil's advocate often shares an opposing or unpopular argument to make others think more deeply about a topic. They may, in fact, disagree with the argument they themselves present.

David does not see his injections of opposing thought as conflicting. He is engaged in the sport of mental gymnastics and loves it. For him, it is a positive trait. Ultimately, this information gathering allows clarification by exploring and looking at all sides of everything. Only some appreciate a healthy debate. Some do not care to see others' points of view at all. Their way of seeing the world is the right and only way.

We have a dear family friend who loves to post inflammatory comments on social media. Politics, economics, religion, there is no topic off-limits; the more contentious, the better. One time, I asked her why she posted these things. She answered that it was fun. It is fun for her, but my children have blocked her from all sites because her comments offended them too many times, which is sad. She is a woman I respect and could be a positive role model for my kids. What she intends to be lively, entertaining banter others find offensive or even hurtful. We have different thresholds on what we consider helpful comments or constructive discussions.

We all know and experience conflict daily. Conflict exists if something or someone is in the way of you getting what you want or expect. Conflict can lurk around the corner when driving down the street, sitting at a desk, or standing in line at the grocery store. One look or one word can derail your plans and your good mood. Your dog wakes you up to go outside thirty minutes before your alarm goes off. You want to turn over and continue snoozing, but you can feel the dog staring at you and hear his tail thumping. Cute Fido is the source of conflict. Not all conflict is bad, however. If Fido did not wake you up to do his business, you would be left with a much bigger and messier problem than missing a few hours of beauty sleep. The uncomfortable tension that may arise from two opposing forces colliding is a warning that there is an issue that needs addressing.

Once we have deemed something an obstacle to what we need or want and recognized it as such, determining how we interpret the situation varies. What one person might see as insurmountable differences another sees as a welcomed challenge. Reactions to disagreements are as numerous as the paint choices at Sherwin-Williams. The shades are as nuanced as the colors of a rainbow. Just watch a couple trying to pick out a shade for the bathroom and listen to the discussion. A heated debate can be a positive exchange of ideas or a personal assault on one's character, depending on how the conversation is presented and received.

So, if our perceptions regarding conflict differ, how can we begin to agree on a definition? I asked friends and family for their definitions of conflict. Their answers were very similar:

- Two or more people thinking differently.
- Argument, disagreement
- Difference of opinion or perspective
- Clarifying conversation between people who have differing viewpoints
- Aggressive presumptions or assumptions

I asked the same people if they had ever experienced a time when they felt a disagreement or argument had gone too far, so the conversation was no longer productive. If so, what were the indicators that an argument had crossed a line into dangerous territory? Here are their responses, and this time, they were markedly different:

- Raised voices
- Disrespectful, hurtful, personal statements or verbal attacks
- Name-calling
- Emotionally charged, "Hot headed"
- Non-listeners, unwilling to listen to other views, closed-minded
- The other person(s) doesn't respect your opinion and tries to change your mind suggesting your opinion is wrong.
- One person shuts down and ends the conversation.
- Only one person shares their views, so it is never clear what the other person is thinking.

We each have varying thresholds for when a conversation or situation crosses into conflict, but we know it when it happens. We are no longer participating in an exchange of words and ideas. Positions and viewpoints can seem as far apart as the depth and width of the Grand Canyon. Vocal tone and physical postures change. Responses are visceral–a whole-body experience. Chests tighten, heart rates increase, fists clench, and necks stiffen as postures alter and the body prepares for battle.

In my mid-thirties, I hosted a small group of women who met monthly to eat and "pray" together. The "praying" often was more gossip and venting than petitioning God, but that can be a slippery slope. One evening, our discussion turned to dating and how we would prepare our young children for this rite of passage. One friend shared that she and her husband instructed their children that when looking for potential partners to look for someone who was their equal or better. She explained that when they looked for their lifelong mate, they needed to look for someone with a skin color the same as theirs, "the closer the color, the better." At that moment, I felt like someone had sucker-punched me in the stomach. There was an immediate visceral reaction to her words, physical and primal. My frontal cortex went offline. All thought was gone.

What is it?

I was appalled by her nonchalant admission of racial prejudice: skin color was a prerequisite for equality. I was in shock. Without thought, I stood up, almost knocking my chair over. The red-hot feeling started at my toes and shot out of me and through my mouth like volcanic lava. I spewed, "We do not speak like that in this house! I can't believe you said that!" One friend giggled at my reaction. Another pretended it didn't happen. And as quickly as I had felt the rush of righteous anger, I felt shame and embarrassment for my outburst. I'm not sure exactly what happened next. At some point, I sat back down. The whole exchange felt uncomfortable. It felt wrong. I felt wrong even though I knew logically that I was right to call her out. It wasn't that I felt wrong for my personal conviction. I felt wrong in that I lost control. I lost my temper. I blew my stack. I was embarrassed by my reaction. She had targeted a very deep and fundamental value of mine in my own home, and yet I was the one who felt wrong for reacting.

I was embarrassed because I thought showing anger was wrong.

As a Christian, southern woman, I had been taught ladies do not get angry. Gossip, slander, and snarky asides were acceptable attributes of a lady, but not raised voices or strong gestures. Lama Rod Owens writes of his complicated relationship with anger in his book *Love and Rage*. "Some of us have been conditioned to believe that we're good, and so we don't get angry, or that it's not ladylike to be angry."[6] Owens goes on to say how we often miss the target in our response to anger.

> Sometimes, thinking that we can be skillful in responding to anger is like believing that we can hit a target with a ball after we get twisted and turned around and really dizzy, then trying to hit the target. That's how anger is. We may actually hit the target sometimes, but mostly not.[7]

---

[6] Lama Rod Owens, *Love and Rage: The Path of Liberation Through Anger* (Berkley, California, North Atlantic Books, 2020) 16

[7] Owens, *Love and Rage,* 16

I would love to say my prayer meeting explosion ended with a constructive conversation on interracial marriages. I would love to write that we arrived at a more profound respect for each other's views. I'd really love to say that I spoke eloquently and with such passion that all were changed for the better. Another ending I play out in my head is that I marched her sorry ass out of my house and found a new group of friends. But I didn't. Finding a new group happened slowly over time and never directly or honestly. Many years later, I reflect on how this whole exchange could have gone so much better. I shut down the conversation with my reaction. A chance for real discussion and honest exchange could have happened that night, but no one was brave enough to venture into the turbulent topic after I blew my stack.

If I could rewind and have a do-over, I would go back to that moment when I knew there was a difference of opinion. My friend said something, and I felt a reaction. My insides resembled a cartoon where the steam engine is heating, shaking, and percolating to the point that you know it's about to blow. Was I wrong to feel angry? Is it wrong to express my anger toward another person, especially if the person is a brother or sister in Christ?

The church is one of the first places I received the message that anger is almost always inherently wrong. As a young girl, I heard that I was to forgive someone who had sinned against me 77 times (Matthew 18: 21-22). I learned the fruits of the Spirit: love, joy, peace, patience, kindness, goodness, faithfulness, gentleness, and self-control (Galatians 5:22-23). Peace, patience, and self-control, don't seem to leave room for fighting or taking up a cause. I have attended many Christian conferences and seminars but have never seen a breakout session on "How to Disagree with Fellow Believers in Five Easy Steps" or "How to Take Down Your Foe the Jesus Way." However, I have experienced conflict within churches and with fellow believers, perhaps more than non-believers.

It is hard to connect deeply with brothers and sisters in Christ when there are differing views, opinions, and priorities. Solutions can be extremely challenging even when all have the best intentions. God has given us free will. We each see and perceive the world differently, which is an amazing gift until your perceptions interfere with mine. How to merge all this free will into healthy and fruit-producing relationships is often unclear. The Bible is very clear on dealing with straightforward sins and heresies; differences of opinion are not as obvious.

The definition I received of a good Christian was to be passive, but Jesus was anything but passive. He was always moving against the conventions of the day. He came into the world to show a different way. He came to earth to change it for the better. Change only occurred with Him bucking many preconceived ideas. To do the Father's will, Jesus had to engage in conflict. Sometimes, He responded to conflict, and other times, He instigated it.

In Matthew 23, Jesus insults some Pharisees, calling them whitewashed tombs. In Jesus' day tombs or mausoleums were covered with watered-down white paint. They "look beautiful on the outside but on the inside are full of the bones of the dead and everything unclean." (Matthew 23:27). Jesus compared the spiritual condition of the Pharisees to a pile of decaying and moldering dead bones. This proclamation would have been highly offensive because under Mosaic Law, "Whoever touches the dead body of any person shall be unclean seven days" (Numbers 19:11). Jesus was saying the Pharisees were not only spiritually dead, but they were also unclean, which would have been a huge insult.

The Biblical passage of the woman at the well demonstrates Jesus' boldness in championing the oppressed (John 4:7-42). Not only did He speak to a woman, considered at this time to be a third-class citizen, but also to a Samaritan, whom the Jews believed to be unclean. To be in her presence would then make Jesus unclean. Not only did He speak to her, He asked her for a cup of water. She wouldn't have had a disposable paper cup handy to offer him. He would have had to drink from her same cup. Scandalous!

The Samaritan woman was an outcast even among her people. She was shunned because of her sex, ethnicity, and extensive relationship history, but none of that mattered to Jesus. He saw her need for living water and salvation. Jesus knew this encounter would not go unnoticed. He took her fight upon himself and gave her a way out of her past and limited existence. He knew His choices might engender conflict with many but demonstrated the cost was worth it.

Also consider the story of the woman caught in adultery about to be stoned. Jesus stops the crowd of accusers by saying, "Let anyone of you who is without sin be the first to throw a stone at her." (John 8:7) Again, he took her fight upon himself. He faced a group of angry people ready for physical violence. He didn't have to, but he did. Why?

Jesus was consistent and purposeful in his actions, even knowing his actions could ignite controversy or condemnation. Jesus used these situations as opportunities to teach his followers and the religious leaders, moving against law and tradition when needed. He fought to free the oppressed. All His actions pointed people to God and salvation. We also know that Jesus could get mad, like turning the tables over mad.

> When Jesus expresses anger, it is always with a view toward defending and protecting something good or someone he loves. Perhaps this is why he refers to himself as a physician. "Those who are well have no need of a physician, but those who are sick," Jesus said (Mark 2:17). Part of what it means to be a good physician is to be angry at and opposed to injuries, bacteria, viruses, cancers, and other invasive realities that threaten health. As the ultimate good physician, Jesus harnessed righteous anger and resolved to fight the most invasive threat to human flourishing – the reality of sin itself.[8]

---

[8] Scott Sauls, *A Gentle Answer: Our "Secret Weapon" in An Age Of Us Against Them*, (Nashville, Tennessee: Nelson Books, 2020) 109

The disciples also had their fair share of quarrels and squabbles. Bless their sweet little hearts. One of their recurring arguments was over who was responsible for meals. Why didn't they assign someone the specific job of packing lunches? (John 6:5, Mark 8:16, John 4:8) I could have been so helpful. I always remember food!

The disciples also argued over who was the greatest among them. (Luke 9:46-47, Mark 9:33-34; Matthew 18:1) The disputes didn't end with Christ's resurrection, far from it. At the beginning of Acts 15, there is disagreement over Gentiles needing to be circumcised and follow the laws of Moses. The final six verses of the chapter recount a dispute between Paul and Barnabas. Ultimately, the argument leads Paul and Barnabas to part ways. Ironically, Paul wrote in Philippians 2:14, "Do everything without complaining and arguing." In 2 Timothy 2:14, Paul instructed the church leaders to "keep reminding God's people. Warn them before God against quarreling about words; it is of no value and only ruins those who listen." It is oddly comforting that Paul wrestled with his humanity just like the rest of us. I suspect, like me, he had to learn the hard way, through lots of trial and error.

Conflict is inevitable. It is an unavoidable part of life. Jesus experienced it. The disciples engaged in it. The early church was rife with it. Is there a way to prepare ourselves so that our responses are constructive, instructive, and edifying? Can we head off heated exchanges before they happen, like preventative medicine or periodic system checks for a car? Is there a way to catch and interrupt potential harmful interactions before they occur? Can we reduce the casualties from clashing ideas and opinions? Can we turn negative interactions into positive ones? And herein lies the hope of this book: preparing ourselves for life's inevitable conflicts so that we can engage in healthy, productive conversations.

I learned in an English class long ago that you can't have literary drama without conflict. Hang with me. I'm not going to teach an English lesson. There is a point to the literary reference. Conflict is a literary device characterized by a struggle between two opposing forces.

We have all read books and watched TV shows and movies. We share experiences through these vehicles of entertainment. These genres are central to our lives and a shared universal experience.

I am using the literary definition of conflict as the definition used in this book because it is familiar to most: a struggle between two or more opposing forces.

The climactic plot structure is familiar because we don't just experience it as passive audience members. We live out the climatic design every day of our lives. Art reflects life, and I use this simple design to illustrate a complex topic. The climactic plot structure is this: opposing forces clash until one significant catalyst ultimately leads to a resolution. Within one day, we may each have many different sub-plots, tiny little scenes playing out each day, or one day may have a more extensive plot line. We can also have an ongoing saga that never seems to resolve, or the resolution takes days, weeks, or even years to come to fruition. There are some conflicts that feel never-ending. Here is a visual illustration of the climatic structure.

Climax Plot Structure

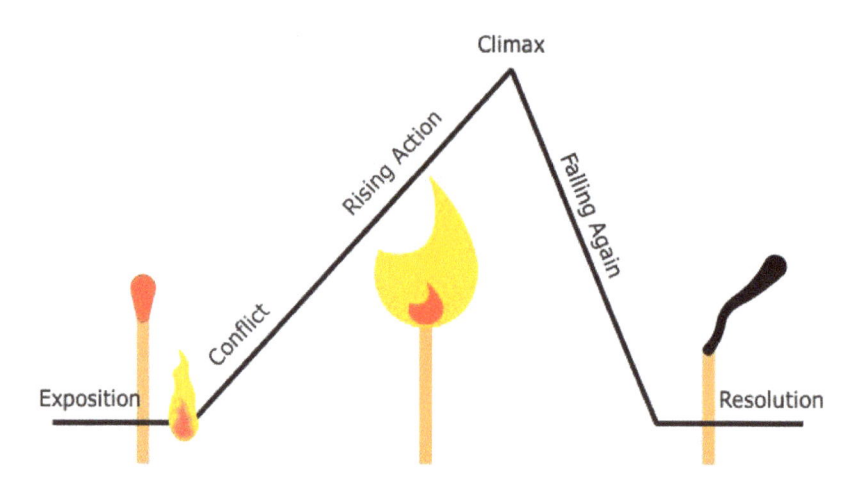

What is it?

The exposition establishes the character and setting. We are introduced to the people involved in the story. That little flame in the diagram is called the ***inciting incident***. It is critically important as it is what sets everything in motion. A match isn't dangerous. It's just a match. A flame isn't dangerous if used wisely. Fire in fact is what sets humans apart from the animal world, but fire also has the potential to be incredibly destructive. The strike of a match has a familiar sound and smell. You can close your eyes and recall the feel of the match striking a rough surface, you feel the friction, hear the match head ignite, and feel the first moments of intense heat. In much the same way, we recall what it is to be in the moment when two or more forces clash. We know how it feels in our bodies. The inciting incident is what sets the conflict in motion. The rising action on the diagram occurs as the tension between opposing forces increases. During rising action phase, more of the conflict is understood and revealed. All of the tension and heightened emotional responses build to the highest point culminating in the climax. At the climax it becomes obvious how the story is going to end: a physical fight, a compromise, a declaration of a winner, a divorce, a murder, a reconciliation. The falling action is when tensions ease slightly as the situations created by the conflict are wrapped up. And, finally, there is the resolution, that little bit at the end that ties up all the loose ends.

That little flame on the diagram above is critical. The flame marks the *inciting incident*. It is the moment that sets everything in motion. It's the event that kicks off the plot and starts the conflict. Something happens that upsets the main character's world. So, what is "it" exactly? "It" is the prelude to the battle. "It" is the spark before the fire. "It" is the bell before the fight. You get the idea.

> Between stimulus and response there is a space. In that space is our power to choose our response. In our response lies our growth and freedom.[9]

---

[9] Owens, *Love and Rage*, XIV

In the words of Supreme Court Justice Potter Stewart, when struggling to define pornography, "....I know it when I see it."[10] What brings us to the fight will vary. What keeps us in the arena will change from person to person, but we know when we move from spectator to participant. We know "it" when we experience it.

How prepared are you for the "it" that potentially could upset your world? How can you start planning and preparing for things that may or may not happen? How can you plan for the unknown? The climatic structure starts with the exposition, establishing the characters and setting. Let's start there. You have been cast as the main character in your life. Congratulations! You're the star!

Reflection/Discussion Questions:

- How do you define conflict?
- What is your "whole body experience" when conflict happens? What do you feel and where in your body do you feel it?
- Can you relate to Kristy's experience at the prayer group with her friend? How do you think you might have reacted? What similar experiences have you had?
- How does the Climactic Structure in literature help you think about the conflict in your own life?

---

[10] Peter Latman, "The Origin of Justice Stewart's 'I Know It When I See It,'" *Wallstreet Journal*, (Sept. 27, 2007)

Chapter 2

The Main Character

Choosing authenticity is not an easy choice. E.E. Cummings wrote, "To be nobody-but-yourself in a world which is doing its best, night and day, to make you everybody but yourself – means to fight the hardest battle which any human being can fight – and never stop fighting." "Staying real" is one the most courageous battles that we'll ever fight.[11]

HAVE YOU EVER had one of those days when you just wake up angry? Before the day even starts, the littlest thing frustrates you. You don't know why, but you feel mad at everything and everyone. Have you ever wanted to punch something? I mean, not a person just, you know, something? Anything! A couch cushion maybe? Better yet, a punching bag. I've heard there are exercise classes where everyone gets their own punching bag. Loud music plays, and you get to hit the bag as hard as you can. Doesn't it sound like it would feel so good just to let loose on a punching bag until you were spent and exhausted? No? Just me? Hmmmm. I think I might have missed my calling. I think I might have been good at boxing. Just saying.

    I've done some great cardio workouts doing kickboxing. Thankfully, there were no mirrors where I could see myself because I thought I

---

[11] Brene Brown, *The Gifts of Imperfection: 10th Anniversary Edition*, (New York, Random House, 2010) 69

looked pretty fierce. I'm not sure reality would stand up to the image I had in my head. Once I got in the zone and my adrenaline kicked in, I created a whole scenario in my head about who I was boxing. My heart rate increased as I jabbed, hooked, and kicked. In my fantasy, I could see my opponent facing me, eyes partially covered by headgear, sweat dripping down her face. The concentration was evident by the look in her razor-focused eyes. Her mouth clenched tight with lips stretched over a mouthguard as we circle each other. The ropes surrounding the mat blur as I hone all my attention to the foe in front of me. I know spectators are there, but my focus is on the enemy of the moment. When I get mad, I can get the same tunnel vision as Laila Ali, the boxing champion and daughter of Muhammad Ali. My adrenaline kicks in, and I feel like I could "Float like a butterfly. Sting like a bee. You can't hit what your eyes don't see."

The irony of my focus being on my opponent is that the only thing I have control over in any fight is myself. I am concentrating on her, yet I can't control my opponent. I don't know what she will do, especially since she's not actually real. If this were a real fight, I could respond to the blows after they happen, but the only part of the fight I can own are my punches and counters.

It's interesting how much we focus on others when in conflict, believing the problem is all theirs, often blinded to our contributions to rising tensions. We try to change the other person…change their minds…change their behaviors. If only they would listen and understand how right I am! How effective have you ever been at changing someone else?

It's easy to see the splinter in someone else's eye and miss the log in our own. (Matthew 7:5)

> This is the human tendency to look outward for explanations rather than inward. You can find this response as early as the third chapter of Genesis: Adam blames Eve and God, and Eve blames the serpent. The blame

game has been one of our favorite responses to anxiety ever since. Anxious systems do a lot of finger-pointing. People see themselves as victimized rather than taking responsibility for their own attitudes and behaviors. Members (Church members –my addition) engage constantly in diagnosing others, focusing on what is wrong with others. Ironically, this refusal to look inward and take responsibility also prevents people from looking inward to see the strengths God has given them to deal with life. The blame game keeps them from thinking about taking responsibility for themselves.[12]

Before a boxer engages in an actual match, a lot of preparation must occur, including conditioning, training, strategy, diet, and practice. Before we engage in conflict, we need to prepare ourselves. Before engaging in an argument, we must develop plans before facing any perceived enemy. One of the first steps is to focus more on ourselves than our opponent. I think about relationships where I concentrated more on the faults of others than I did my own. In truth, I was so weak in self-reflection and self-examination that I wasn't aware of many of my shortcomings, or it might have been that I didn't want to face my faults. It was much easier to see the speck in someone else's eyes. The log in mine was too hard to move, so I didn't even try until I had no choice.

You may be reading this in frustration because you picked up this book hoping to gain ninja-like skills in verbal combat. What on earth does knowing yourself have to do with conflict? You didn't sign up for therapy. You don't need a book on personal growth or self-reflection. After all, you think the problem isn't you; it's them. Oh, my young Padawan (Star Wars student reference), you must learn the truth about yourself before the force can be great in you. Seriously, the only person

---

[12] Jim Herrington, R. Robert Creech, and Trisha Taylor, *The Leader's Journey: Accepting the Call to Personal and Congregational Transformation*, (San Francisco, Jossey-Bass, 2003) 64

you can control when it comes to conflict is yourself. I am so sorry if that is news to you. Maybe you were hoping to learn how to control the thoughts and opinions of others. The reality is that you can only control *your* thoughts, opinions, and actions. You cannot control anyone else. Why am I starting with us taking a hard look at ourselves? Because that's where the secret sauce is. I promise we are going to get to the other guy. We will talk about "them" and deal with others later, but first we are going to take a long hard look in the mirror. Are you the person you want to be in the face of extreme stress and obstacles? We have more power over conflict than we think, but it's not outside us. It is in us. So, we need to ask some questions. Who am I? What are my priorities? What is most important to me? What are my beliefs and values?

I recently had an experience that crystallized what I deem most important and also witnessed my husband David's life values in action. Fact is stranger than fiction, and this is what happened. My husband and I took our grandkids to Chic-Fil-A a few days ago. I am truly sorry if you don't have a Chic-Fil-A where you live. There really is something amazing about their food and service. If you are on a road trip and pass one, it is worth the stop. Anyway, we took the kids, ages 6, 3, and 18 months to this Chic-Fil-A. It is summertime and well over 100 degrees. We are Texans, but it takes its toll on everyone when it is legitimately over 100 degrees multiple days in a row. You do feel everyone is a bit on edge. The baby had overheated in the car despite the AC being on full blast. She was crying and miserable. I rescued her from her car seat while David wrangled the other two from their different seat contraptions.

We walked into the restaurant with this pathetic baby crying, curls sticking to her sweaty head. The two boys bounced more than walked beside us. I'm blowing on the sweet baby, taking off her shoes, and doing anything I can to cool her down. The 6-year-old is pulling off his shoes and running for the enclosed play area; his brother is close behind. I'm loudly reminding the younger one to take off his shoes while consoling baby girl and giving Pop-Pop (David/grandfather) instructions on food and drink orders. While still holding my plump, sweaty bundle, I clumsily maneuver a highchair to a table. David arrives with drinks when I see the three-year-old has not removed his shoes. I briskly move to the glass-enclosed play area and open the heavy glass door to the playground, only to realize that my grandson has peed all over himself. His shorts are soaked. I have no change of clothes for him. Still holding baby girl, I enter the play area and quietly ask him to come with me, not wanting to draw more attention to him. Thankfully, he came peacefully. As I get to our table, I tell David the situation, wanting him to commiserate and brainstorm our next move. He, however, is very distracted.

I want to interject that David is a full-on, engaged grandfather, ika Pop-Pop. We have been married for 35 years. I know him well, and all I knew at that moment was that he was acting weird. Weird enough that it trumped the predicament I found myself in with my left arm numb from holding a chunky babe and my right hand holding tight to the wet pant boy. Just then, our food arrives, which interrupts my questioning David's strange demeanor. I told the pee-clad boy to sit down, and yes, we cleaned the chair later. I instinctively knew not to question David about what was happening. Without making eye contact with me, David helps me dole out the food and get everyone situated, but David is looking past me. I swear he looks like a dog on point. He is very intent and razor-focused on something behind me. I know something is off, and the hairs stand up on the back of my neck.

Without looking at me, he slides the keys toward me and tells me I should take the kids to the van if needed. I, being the obedient godly wife, think, holy heck! How am I supposed to get these three kids in a van? One has his shoes off and is currently suspended in the air in a life-sized car in an enclosed glassed room with a ridiculously heavy door; another is walking like he just got off of a horse because his shorts and undies are soaked through, and the other was just traumatized by the very van you want me to put her in! Are you kidding me?! I cannot contain myself any longer. I practically shout, "What? Why? What is going on?"

He whispers to me that there is a group of Aryan Brotherhood at the table next to us. He tells me five men and one woman had shirts with "Aryan by birth. Brotherhood by Choice" written on them. They are sitting directly behind us. They also had AB hats and numerous swastika and SS tattoos on their faces and arms. It wasn't until we got home that I looked up information on the group. The Britannica says the "Aryan Brotherhood, [a] notoriously violent white supremacist group and organized crime syndicate. It is the oldest, largest, and deadliest prison gang in the United States. The neo-Nazi group has a major racist component, but this often is secondary in importance to the consolidation of power and acquisition of profit. The Aryan Brotherhood's criminal enterprises include extortion, narcotics trafficking, murder, male prostitution, and gambling operations."[13]

The Aryan group got up and left without incident a few minutes after he told me about them. Our reactions may seem alarmist to some, but in our area, there have been shootings and bomb threats. He was right to have reacted the way he did. As I've thought about all that happened in the brief encounter, I realize how much our previous knowledge of ourselves and each other determined how we responded to the situation.

- I knew I could trust David to discern trouble and protect our grandkids and myself to the best of his ability. I also knew he would not instigate or escalate any conflict.
- I knew I would get those kids to safety or put my body between them and danger without hesitation.
- David's focus was divided, which I didn't understand until later. When we got in the car, he told me there was a young, small Indian girl the men kept watching. He knew I would protect the kids, but he was concerned for a girl he didn't know. She was alone and defenseless and perhaps even unaware of any danger.

---

[13] Metych, M.. "Aryan Brotherhood." Encyclopedia Britannica, January 7, 2024. https://www.britannica.com/topic/Aryan-Brotherhood.

In a split second, without thought, we responded to potential conflict in ways that were true to our character. These decisions of who we were and what was important to us were not decided at the moment but long before. Our trust in each other had deep roots. Our desire to protect the vulnerable had been established long before, and we each knew it was critically important to us. Our calm and calculated demeanor was purposeful, both of us knowing the goal would be to de-escalate the situation. We are never looking for or wanting a fight – anywhere, ever! Neither of us wants to be called upon to be heroic, far from it, but we know our values and priorities. We will intervene, if we feel it is necessary. The way we responded that day was decided long before we entered the Chic-fil-A.

When it comes to conflict, what do you bring to the table? How does your natural disposition fit into emotionally charged exchanges? Are you a natural instigator of needed change? Is your bent more towards peacekeeping or peacemaking? There is a big difference.

Who are you? Loaded question, right? When I ask myself this question, I immediately think I'm a wife, mother, Christian, daughter, sister, and so on, but if I am asked to define myself outside of those labels, I really struggle. There are other labels I can put on myself, such as American, white, and middle class. All of these are true! But they are true of so many other people, so the question remains, **Who am I?** What sets me apart from everyone else? I'm not exactly like everyone else. How has God uniquely created me to be in this world? What sets me apart from others? What sets you apart?

Creating The Garden of You

If you are like most, you have difficulty discerning who you are, separate from the roles you play. I want to take you on an imaginative and creative journey. I want you to design your ideal garden—a place where you would feel comfortable and could flourish. Money is no object. There is no limitation of space or location. What would you want your garden to look like? In America, we think of gardens as flower beds in the front of your house or the raised vegetable gardens in the backyard. Think bigger. In England, gardens refer to a small piece of land usually enclosed by a fence. In America, this would be referred to as a yard. So, think big. What would your ideal outdoor living space look like? In this metaphor, the garden represents your inner world: your thoughts, beliefs, dreams, goals, temperament, personality, values, and preferences. So, what would your garden look like? How would the garden of you be designed? Can you immediately picture it, or does the question leave you baffled?

God has created you with certain gifts. He has wired you in a certain way to fit into the body of Christ as a whole. (1Peter 4:10, 1Corinthians 12:7-12) We are born with a personality, temperament, and disposition. As we navigate life, we learn various coping skills that may alter our personalities, but we are born with a unique way of seeing and being in the world. Have you ever held a newborn baby? Do they have a personality? Some are sleepy. Some are squiggly. Some are alert and seem to look around and respond to noise. Have you ever been in a room with one-year-olds? Do they all behave the same way? What about a room full of two-year-olds? Oh my! These budding little people can be as different and varied as the rose bushes in the Tyler, Texas, Rose Gardens. I am hoping you can unearth who you were created to be.

Don't compare yourselves to others. Don't try on different masks to be who you think you should be or what others have told you to be. This is a time to discover who you are. We will talk about growth and challenging yourself later right now I want to focus on your God-given design. What is your comfort zone or your natural state? When no one is watching, who are you?

Use your imagination to create your garden. You have limitless funds. The location can be anywhere you desire. This garden represents you. God has gifted us with unique personalities: our way of seeing and being in the world. And we are each beautifully and uniquely made. So, let's start there. How has God wired you? What are your personal preferences? Some clues to your inner world might be how you would dress, if money were no object. What would your dream home look like? What colors do you like? Here are just a few garden designs to help get you thinking. Let your imagination play! Have fun with this.

English Garden

Are you more of an English garden with crisp hedges and vertical evergreen accents? Every element is built on symmetry and harmony. Your manicured lawns are beautifully divided by straight paths of crushed granite. Your garden is well-maintained and harmonious. Everything has a place, and each element complements the other.

Has God wired you to be organized and well-prepared for all things? Are you someone who follows through on your commitments and always does a good job? Do you have a keen sense of right and wrong, good and bad? Can you lean into problems and find solutions? I thank God for you because He has not gifted me in these ways. You are needed and a beautiful addition to this chaotic world. May you continue to flourish and keep the rest of us on track!

Cottage Garden

Cottage gardens are charming and inviting. Typically, seating areas are scattered throughout, inviting you to "come and sit a spell." These gardens are more informal and a bit romantic. Ivy grows up walls, and vines hang over trellises. There is no space between big blooming flowers. They are so artfully created that you might think the garden just happened like nature sneezed this cacophony of foliage into being. However, your garden is carefully crafted to be appealing and inviting.

Are you someone who usually has a full calendar and many people in your life? Do you welcome people into your home and almost always have a dessert or casserole in the freezer? Does hospitality come naturally to you? Do you love to be needed and included? You are a great friend to many, and we are so thankful for you. Your encouragement makes us all better. Thank you for your gift of seeing our needs.

Zen Garden

Zen gardens are typically small and enclosed. Zen gardens are structured around seven design rules: austerity, simplicity, naturalness, asymmetry, subtlety, unconventionality, and stillness. They invite meditation and solitude. The elements are sparse and minimalistic. The water features are small and emanate a tranquil sound. Gravel is the preferred ground cover in Zen gardens because it is not easily disturbed by weather or feet.

Are you someone who values your solitude and peace? Does your presence bring a sense of calm? Do people seek you out for your wise counsel? Is your life simple? Must you retreat to gain perspective and energy? Your calendar isn't as full as some, but you operate from a place of inner stability and strength. You are well-liked, but people underestimate what you can accomplish for the greater good. Thank you for seeing what the rest of us miss in our business. We need your calm, peace, and wise words. You are a balm to our souls.

Rooftop Gardens

Rooftop Gardens are all about the view. The higher the building, the better the view. Clear glass barriers are the enclosure for this open space. Sitting areas for multiple people and maybe even a hot tub or sauna might be tucked into the design. These gardens can help to insulate buildings and reduce the temperatures of the floors below. Plant boxes are strategically placed so as not to block the amazing view. There may even be full-grown trees in large planters on the roof.

Ah, the Rooftop gardeners. They bring the fun! They are poised so that they can see what is happening around them. Are you eager to find the next great adventure? Do you love to have parties and go, go, go? Do you think resting is for the weak? Do you feel the more people, the better, because you hate to be alone? You are optimistic and can reframe anything to be positive. Thank God for people like you! You help us not to take ourselves so seriously. You literally drop the temperature and tension in the room. You bring fun into the world, and we are so thankful for you.

Rock Garden

Rock gardens are beautiful in their simplicity, practicality, and are low maintenance. These gardens use native plants and require very little to thrive and grow. Rock gardens typically have strong lines and little ornamentation but are designed with much thought and effort. The great thing about these gardens is that they fluctuate little with the changing seasons. They will look the same in January as they do in July.

Are you steady and strong? Do you like simplicity and predictability? All you need is a good book, a glass of water, and a nice chair to make you happy? People would describe you as stable and predictable. What a gift to a crazy world. You focus on information and knowledge. You research topics tirelessly and are a wealth of information.

Create Your Own Thing

Maybe you don't recognize yourself in these gardens. Don't worry! You can create something entirely different than the ones mentioned. Perhaps you are more like a natural garden: a field of wildflowers needing little maintenance, identifying yourself as a free spirit and a little wild. Most likely, you will see yourself in multiple options. Like me, you may be a combination of a couple of different gardens. Maybe gardening isn't really your thing. That's okay. I chose to use gardens as the metaphor because gardens are easily changed. If a plant doesn't grow well in a particular location, you can move it. If you don't like something you planted or a plant has voluntarily sprung up in your garden uninvited, you can dig it up and throw it in the compost pile. Gardens have different seasons. They change. We change. We grow. We have times when we need more maintenance than others. The cycle of growth is never-ending. We are constantly evolving and growing. Jim Cymbala writes in *Fresh Wind, Fresh Power*, "We are always either drawing nearer to God or falling away; There is no holding pattern."[14] God stays fixed, but we are ever evolving and growing creatures. We are being shaped into Jesus' likeness. "All of us! Nothing between us and God, our faces shining with the brightness of his face. And so we are transfigured much like the Messiah, our lives gradually becoming brighter and more beautiful as God enters our lives and we become like him." (2 Corinthians 3:18)

Perhaps you can't see yourself as a beautiful garden because you feel like your life is overgrown with weeds and thorns. There's been no refreshing rain for weeks, months, or even years. Maybe there is even some old debris here and there that you keep meaning to throw away. Let me say, I am truly sorry. I've been there. Finding your way out of a dying, crowded landscape can be difficult.

As I write this, the area in which I live has had consecutive days of over 100 degrees. Everything is brown and crunchy. It is so hot that walking outside hurts. Even leaves on old established trees are turning brown. You would think all is dead and that nothing will ever grow in this land of drought. Amazingly, however, the rain will fall from the sky at some point, and we will see green again. The rain will come. A verse that I often cling to is, "For His anger is but for a moment, His favor is for life; Weeping may endure for a night, but joy comes in the morning" (Psalm 30:5 NKJV). Joy will come to quench your thirsting and tired soul.

Self-care is critically important to our physical, emotional, and spiritual well-being. Unfortunately, I think we've made self-care too complicated. The phrase "self-care" is one that has been overused. If you did everything suggested by "experts" to keep yourself sane, you would never have time for anything besides taking care of yourself! I heard someone say that self-care is whatever you need to do to make you feel

---

[14] Jim Cymbala with Dean Merrill, *Fresh Wind, Fresh Fire*, (Grand Rapids, Michigan, Zondervan, 2003) 163.

more like yourself. I love that simple definition. It's going to be different for each person. What do you need to do to make you feel more like yourself? Take a bath? Read a book? Go for a walk? Pray? Talk to a friend? It may be a series of things and might take some time. It could be a one-and-done kind of thing or a longer process. Maybe it's just a good night's sleep. Or maybe you need to do some serious excavation before you can even think about God's original design for you? Are you lost in all the weeds? Do you need to do some digging and discarding before you can begin planting? The next chapter deals with just that: excavating. Cling to this hope. Joy does come in the morning.

Reflection/Discussion Questions:

- Do you feel like you are the main character in your story or are there times that it seems someone else is the hero or the villain of your story?
- Who are you? What immediately comes to mind when asked that question? What roles do you play? What labels would apply? Going beyond those, what makes you unique? What makes you "you?"
- Do you see yourself in the gardens that Kristy describes? Are you an English garden or a Zen garden? A cottage garden or a rock garden? A rooftop garden or a natural garden? Is there another kind of garden that comes to mind? Use your imagination to "see" the garden that represents your life. What do you see? Do you believe that is how others see you? How do you feel about what you see?
- In the chapter, we learned that gardens are easily changed— we can move plants to flourish elsewhere, and we can remove plants that don't belong. How is your own life-garden changing? What changes would you like to make?
- Kristy writes, "Self-care is whatever you need to do to feel more like yourself." What things do you do (or could you do) that

make you feel more like yourself? As the main character of your own story, could you create more space for those things? How will you write self-care into your story?

Chapter 3

Emotional Excavation

Lord, let our labors in this garden be fruitful.
Lord, let our labors in this garden be blessed.[15]

THE MOST CHALLENGING part of gardening is the preparation of the soil: the back-breaking work of cracking hard ground, throwing out rocks, pulling up weeds, and building a fence to keep out predators. Before a flower blooms or fruit appears, there is much work.

Many years ago, my husband and I had to have a new aerobic septic system put into our backyard. A huge hole was dug for a large tank to be inserted into the ground. Trenches for the drainage pipes stretched far out into the corners of our lawn. It looked like wild hogs and super-mutated armadillos had gotten together for a party. Our whole backyard was basically uprooted and ugly. Two large metal lids stuck out of the ground, sorely showing the existence of waste churning underneath. Our yard was not attractive. Being creative and resourceful, I hid evidence of our sewage system with a beautiful garden. My plans were quite extravagant and expensive. The plants were carefully thought out so there would be something blooming at all times. We planted a large palm tree, bushes, and flowers to attract butterflies. We worked hard in the garden, and our labors were worth it. It was beautiful. You could see no evidence of a sewage system. All was hidden.

---

[15] Douglas Kaine McKelvey, *Every Moment Holy, Vol 1*, (Nashville, Rabbit Room Press, 2019) 95

As we were putting in the last plants, clouds were rolling in. How wonderful! Rain for the newly planted garden. It rained and rained, and then it rained some more. It rained for days. Late one afternoon, I walked across the living room floor when something out the window caught my eye. Instead of the rainwater coming down, it was going up. What in the world?! I ran out onto our deck to see a broken pipe spewing raw sewage all over our yard. The huge septic tank had broken free from the ground and was emerging from the earth like a submarine surfacing from the ocean. The tank bounced on top of all the water that had accumulated underneath. It was like a cork popping on a bottle of champagne, but I assure you there was no celebration at our house. As the tank came out of the ground, the whole garden slid beneath it. It was like watching a vast sinkhole swallow all my beautiful plants.

I learned two valuable lessons that day that I'd like to share with you.

1. If you don't deal with your crap properly, it will come to the surface, and usually when you least want it to.
2. You can't make shit pretty or smell good. Don't even try.

Proper Disposal of Waste

For much of my young adult life, I denied my inner world. My self-reflection resembled a heart monitor that had flatlined. There wasn't much thought about what I was feeling or experiencing—all those years of being invisible left me remarkably attuned to others but not myself. My actions and thoughts were only reactions to the thoughts and feelings of others. I was what others expected and wanted. I learned early in life that others wanted me to be agreeable, funny, and productive. Therefore, that is what I was. The charade that was me, appearing to have it all together–securing my mask tightly each day–was how I presented myself to the world. Over time, the mask had been in place for so long that it had adhered to my face and become a constant fixture I didn't even know was there. It wasn't until I hit the wall of deep depression that I had to face some hard truths about myself and deal with my inner world.

With the help of medication, counseling, and a few trusted friends, I began the, often painful, excavation process of self-discovery. It took time, intention, and effort to dig my way out.

Digging Deep

When I was a mother of two adolescent girls, I was doing the best I knew how to do to survive the rigors of parenting. My children were in middle school and dealing with their own stuff–crooked teeth, poor eyesight, acne, etc. Our gene pool is rough. They were finding their way through their complicated young world, going through the painful growing process of separating from their parents. I was experiencing what it was to pour time and energy into these little souls but getting no credit and increasingly less control. On top of this, we had an extra child move in with us for a short time. I was stretched thin, too thin. I increasingly felt….not right.

On the outside, my life looked pretty great, and I did have a good life. So why the lack of enthusiasm? Why the lack of energy? Why so glum? It made no sense. I tried to ignore the feeling and push through the pain.

Eventually, I was unmotivated to do anything at all and had to face that something was wrong. I was depressed. Depressed is not necessarily sad. Depressed is a dark pit you slowly slide into, and no matter how hard you try, you can't climb out. It swallows you whole. It is a dark, black, empty void. The effects of depression are physical. I was bone-weary and tired all of the time. I slept a lot during that time but never felt rested. What was worse than the physical symptoms and the lack of motivation was that I didn't know why I was depressed. I promise you I did not know what was happening inside of me. "Everything is good. Why am I depressed?" I would cry into a pillow so no one would hear.

I did try to talk to people about how I was feeling. The advice friends and family gave me included things like listening to praise music or memorizing scripture. These were not helpful suggestions for someone who could barely get out of bed each day. Their responses to my profound funk were a mix of awkward discomfort and even disbelief. I didn't appear depressed, they would say. Of course, not! I was taught at a very early age to hide emotions. Don't be too high or too low, just steady and pleasant. Don't show others your weakness. Don't allow others to see the mess of your life. A shiny outer appearance is one of the best attributes someone can possess. These were my childhood messages.

When I was about nine, my mother was hospitalized while recovering from a hysterectomy. In those days hysterectomies were performed differently. The uterus was removed through a long incision across the abdomen. I am told recovery was long and painful. I missed my mother. I had not been to the hospital to see her because I was told she was too sick for me to visit. I can only imagine the possible scenarios my little girl mind had conjured up, trying to comprehend what was happening. I remember being home one evening with my father, sister, and grandmother. I was so sad. I just wanted reassurance that everything would be okay and that my mother would return home soon. I started to cry, and my grandmother reached for me. I leaned in, expecting to be embraced, but instead, she covered my face with my hair and told me not to cry because it made me look ugly. This was one of the first lessons instructing me to keep my ugliness and feelings buried deep within.

If my mother were alive, she would tell me not to include my grandmother's story in this book. Of course, this would be her response! The hair-hiding lady raised her. The apple doesn't fall far from the tree. She is another source of my emotional stuffing: my mother. Ironically, my mother processed the world through her emotions, but, like me, she was told feelings were messy and ugly. My mother only expressed emotions at home behind closed doors. Often, her feelings would seep out in unexpected and hurtful ways. Were these women, my grandmother and mother, heartless monsters? Not at all. I was wildly loved and adored. I knew I had two women who would protect me fiercely to the point of death. They were doing the best they could with what tools they had available to them. Tools that, I'm sure, were passed down to them from previous generations.

They passed the same coping tools on to me, and I, in turn, passed them on to my girls. I wanted to raise strong, independent women, and I succeeded in doing just that. There were two phrases I often repeated to my children. "No drama, only theatre" and "suck it up, buttercup." I indeed wanted them to be strong, but in the process, I delivered the same message my matriarchs had given me: showing emotions makes you weak and vulnerable. The subtext: emotions are wrong and ugly.

I have apologized to my children numerous times for not letting them express their emotions freely. I wish I had listened openly to their struggles with friends, teachers, and coaches instead of cutting them short and moving them along too quickly to resolutions. I wish I had sat with them and validated what they were feeling because emotions are important, and they do matter.

Rehashing this story through the lens of conflict has helped me clarify my aversion to confrontation. The childhood message that emotions are bad and unpredictable led to my instinct to run from any conversation that seemed too emotional or uncomfortable. I'm uncomfortable with my own emotions as well as the big feelings of others. Our childhood stories are pivotal in understanding ourselves. Not only had I received the "ugly and messy" message. I also heard that my opinions were not valid and didn't matter. No one wanted to hear them. And, so, I learned to keep my opinions to myself.

I can now say, I am so thankful God allowed me to fall into the pit of depression. That long, dark road was the best thing that could have happened to me. As I clawed my way up, one grip at a time, I discovered who I was created to be. I no longer squelched my thoughts. Alone, I began to journal and heard a tiny sound way deep inside me and for the first time I discovered something. I had a voice. I had my view of the world. It was frightening but so liberating. Through time and intentionality, I found myself and who I was separate from others. And for the most part, I liked her. I recognized that God had made me for "such a time as this," and so has He made you.

Now that you have designed your garden based on your personality and unique wiring, it is time to intentionally clear out some weeds and make room for new growth. What childhood messages have you received that influence how you view and engage in conflict? You may not realize how many of those stories are rolling around in your head and heart and how much they impact the way you view the world. We all have inherited baggage we unwillingly pick up and carry into adulthood. "Personal bias refers to learned beliefs, opinions, or attitudes that people are unaware of and often reinforce stereotypes. These personal biases are unintentional, automatic, and inbuilt, leading to incorrect judgments."[16]

In Beth Moore's memoir, she writes of her relationship with her family:

> These are my people. My original loves, my flesh and my bones. I know their jokes. I know their quirks. We have the same noses. Different slices of the same secrets on our plates. We've survived the same blows. We speak in strange tongues, syllables of a run-on sentence that began in our infancies, untranslatable to casual visitors. All my knotted-up life I've longed for the sanity and simplicity of knowing who's good and who's bad…This was not theological. It was strictly relational. God could do what he wanted with eternity. I was just trying to make it here in the meantime, and what I thought would help me make it was for people to be one thing or the other, good or bad.[17]

---

[16] "What are Examples of Personal Biases," Impactly, Inc. https://getimpactly.com

[17] Beth Moore, *All My Knotted-Up Life: A Memoir*, (Carol Stream, Illinois, Tyndale House Publishers, 2023) 14

Very early in life, we learn coping skills to help make life more manageable for our young brains. Children are sponges, taking in all the messages around them. What "truths" did you absorb before you developed the ability to think for yourself? Who did you define as good? What were the characteristics of bad people? Perhaps a message you received was, "Cleanliness is next to godliness" or people who smell bad and don't dress to Sunday church standards are lazy, disrespectful, and, most likely, dangerous. As an adult, you know that being clean is a privilege. It costs money to be clean. Not everyone has the same access to water, soap, and laundry, but still, when you see or smell someone who doesn't measure up to your standards, the idea that they are lazy creeps in. You cross to the other side of the street when you see someone who looks unkempt. Perhaps your childhood message was bent in another direction.

> Like many folks who grew up blue-collar, we didn't think much of rich people. Growing up, we felt it was okay to look down our noses on people who had lots of money. We weren't allowed to harbor prejudices about anyone else. We were taught that people of all races, nationalities, and religions were to be respected. But people with money were "those" people.
>
> No one actually said they were bad people, but some subliminal message told us that wealth and greed were sinful partners. Being rich wasn't something to admire or aspire to. In a strange way, we almost glorified poverty. "Blessed are the poor in spirit" became "Blessed are the poor."[18]

---

[18] Regina Brett, *Be the Miracle: 50 Lessons for Making the Impossible Possible*, (New York, Grand Central Publishing, 2012) 154

Who are your "those people?" We all have personal biases. If you are like me, you can name a few. People you avoid. They make you uncomfortable. Maybe you pretend not to see them in the store or go out of your way to avoid them. You don't really know them or their story, but somehow, you know they don't fit into your social circle.

These personal biases affect us and how we interact with people. We can be defensive or primed for hate without consciously knowing we feel this way. The only way to get rid of these false narratives is to dig them up and bring them into the light. It takes courage to share what you know to be your "junk" but saying it out loud to someone can help bring clarity. Our prejudices formed early in life can be extremely hard to eliminate. Roots go down deep. You might attend a seminar on erasing prejudicial thinking only to catch yourself returning to the same thought pattern on the way home. Weeds will choke out the good plants, but the more viable and healthy plants you put in your garden, the fewer weeds can grow. Keep going. Keep trying.

All of these thoughts and feelings from our past were hard-wired into our brains. The good news is that our brains are malleable. You can teach an old dog a new trick. We can change our thinking and our behavior.

> This means our histories don't get to impose themselves on us like prophecies. We don't have to be who we've always been.
>
> Whether we've had four years of spiritual sterility or forty, that blockage can be removed. We can embrace a new pattern of abiding, and the life force of the Spirit can flow through our branches, making us astoundingly fruitful.[19]

---

[19] Beth Moore, *Chasing Vines: Finding Your Way to an Immensely Fruitful Life*, (Carol Stream, Illinois, Tyndale House Publishers, 2019) 221

Out with Old

My daughter is a licensed therapist. In 2020, amid a global pandemic and a national shutdown, I asked her how she was coping with the increased demands for therapists. Due to all the turmoil happening in the world, her schedule was always full. People were waiting weeks to see a counselor. Thanks to Zoom, she was still able to meet with most clients. She has always enjoyed working with children, and I wondered how she could do this via a computer screen.

She paused and said, "Actually, I'm seeing a lot of middle school girls and middle-aged men. It seems I have found my niche. It turns out middle-aged men have much in common with middle school girls." My response was laughter. I thought this was hilarious. It was obvious to me that middle school girls are dealing with raging hormones, disconnection from friends, and too much time at home, but what did they have in common with middle-aged men? She explained that all the political unrest, economic insecurities, and pandemic uncertainties were wildly shaking middle-aged men. The men had anger issues, and their wives sent them to counseling. Once again, I laughed. She explained that adolescent girls and men in their 50's – 60's were so angry. They were acting out, and it often came out as uncontrolled rage. Neither adolescent girls, nor grown men know how to deal with all they are feeling. She said, "Many men think the only acceptable emotion for them to express is anger. These grown men will come into my office and start talking. All I have to do is ask them a few questions. I tell them it is okay to feel what they're feeling. I take away the shame surrounding their emotions. It doesn't take long before they are bawling like babies." I stopped laughing. Middle-aged men struggling with emotions wasn't funny. It was heartbreaking.

Grown men need permission to feel emotions. Isn't that crazy? At some point, these men had received the message that anger was the only acceptable emotion. It is intriguing that anger, as a woman, is the only emotion I feel wrong expressing. These hidden messages have huge implications for how we deal with conflict.

A husband and wife might each blame the other for their dwindling savings account. The husband may resent the wife's expenditures or even fear they do not have the security of savings. He doesn't know how to tap into those emotions, so he does the one thing he knows to do: lashes out at his wife. The wife is angry that she is the one who is always blamed for their finances, but instead of expressing her anger, she stuffs it. She becomes sullen and depressed, which causes her husband's frustration to grow, which comes out as anger. Rinse and repeat. The pattern continues. When we react the same way over and over, it is likely in response to messages received in our past. A common saying is, "If it's hysterical, it's most likely historical." If the reaction is over the top, it might just be an old wound that has never been given a chance to heal. All of us have adaptive strategies from our family of origin. One tool in helping to unearth these messages is to pay attention to your emotions. Emotions are indicators of what is going on underneath the surface.

What past messages about emotions must you uncover in your life? What is your default emotional setting when it comes to dealing with opposition? Are you quick to defend yourself, perhaps to the point of being too defensive? Do you find anger right beneath the surface, looking for any excuse to come out, or do you go in the opposite direction and run from any perceived controversy?

Once you see a pattern of behavior, ask yourself why. For me, my emotions came out without my permission. They leaked out. They came out sideways and awkwardly. My reactions were often either bigger or smaller than situations warranted. Why? This question led to my discovery of my childhood programming of stuffing emotions.

At the beginning of the chapter, I shared about my battle with depression. Everything turned around for me when an older-than-me woman saw I was struggling. She took the time to really listen to me. She caught me in a moment of raw desperation and recognized I was lost and hurting. She sat me down and started asking me questions.

Together, we began to unpack what was happening. In a shaky voice, I told her that when it was getting close to the time for my kids to come home from school, I felt..... she didn't let me finish. She interrupted, saying, "You feel a sense of dread and exhaustion. You feel like you can't keep doing all the things day after day?" I looked back at her and, for the first time in a long time, felt completely seen and understood. She courageously shared with me that when she was in my season of life, she kept a box of donuts in her bottom desk drawer at work. She would buy a dozen on the way to work each morning under the guise of planning to share them with her colleagues. In reality, she saved the donuts for herself until the end of the day, when her day job was done, but the night job of parenting was just beginning. She shared that she would stuff donut after donut into her mouth, trying to fill an empty void she felt. She did this for years. She patiently asked me a few questions and listened to my answers. In just a few minutes, this gracious friend gave me hope through her transparent and vulnerable sharing. I clung to her story as if grasping onto a rope as I dangled off the side of a cliff. I was not alone, but I did need help. With her encouragement, I went to see my primary care physician.

My doctor listened intently, put a soft hand on my arm, looked me in the eye, and said, "I see many women experiencing what you have described daily." She confirmed that I was not alone in my struggle. She prescribed an antidepressant for me, and I will be forever grateful. I needed the medicine to help me climb out of my pit. I needed the prescribed medication before determining what was happening inside me. It didn't stop the pain, but it allowed me a little distance so I could actually deal with my internal turmoil. Healing takes time, intentionality, and effort. But it is worth it.

After starting medication, the hard work began. I began to feel. I began to name and understand my emotions. I no longer stuffed what I was feeling. Some things were buried deep within. I persisted until my pattern of dealing with emotions began to change. It still takes effort to understand what I am feeling now. The years of learned behavior take time to change. I have learned skills for dealing with emotions. I am still a work in progress. I especially shy away from big emotions that make me feel out of control. Just like weeding a garden is never-ending, so is the excavation of our emotions.

Before we can understand the emotions of others and deal with "those" people, we first must understand our stories and deal with our stuff. One of the best ways is to recognize our emotions. Emotions are not a nuisance; they are necessary. They give us many clues to the bigger picture of what is happening inside us. Did you know that those big, beautiful trees outside your window have root systems three to five times bigger than the branches, limbs, and visible leaves? Isn't that amazing? God is a magnificent Creator. We haven't even begun to understand the intricacies and vastness of our minds. Don't run from the God-given warning system of what is happening deep down in the roots of your being. Embrace them! Give them names. Understand how they present in your body, allow yourself to feel them, and continue to dig down to the root. It is hard work, and it is ongoing.

> As we cultivate gentle order,
> training,
> pruning,
> weeding,
> and protecting.
> So cultivate and train our wayward hearts,
> O Lord, that rooted in you the forms of
> our lives might spread in winsome witness,
> maturing to bear the good fruit of grace, expressed
> in acts of compassionate love.[20]

---

[20] McKelvey, *Every Moment Holy*, 95

Reflection/Discussion Questions:

- As Kristy's longtime friend, I remember the day that the septic tank popped out of the ground. It was as tragically hilarious as it sounds in her story. Have you learned the two lessons that she learned that day? How are you dealing with your crap? Is it coming to the surface without your permission? How are you trying to make it pretty or smell good?
- Kristy said that she learned early in life that others wanted her to be "agreeable, funny, and productive." How would you finish this sentence: I learned early in life that others wanted me to be _____?
- Kristy described learning in her family that emotions are ugly and messy. How did your family view emotion? What emotions were acceptable to feel and express? What emotions were off-limits?
- Like the roots of a tree in a garden, emotions may be hard to see but are necessary and important. What emotions are you ready to let yourself feel? Can you name them here? How might those emotions help you understand yourself and God a little better?

Chapter 4

Name Them and Claim Them

Emotions are consistently cast as the opposition in a war that never seems to end. The scorched earth of your heart bears the scars, but your heart was never meant to be a battlefield. Your heart is a garden.[21]

YOUR BOSS COMES flying into your office with the report you just sent him in his hands. His face is red, and his shoulders are up around his ears. Your shoulders rise to your ears, mirroring his body posture—your heart rate increases, and sweat puddles in your armpits. You recognize you feel defensive, anxious, and even angry. You spent hours on that report! It wasn't even really your responsibility. You were trying to help out a co-worker. How do you respond as the boss enters? Choose the answer you feel is best for the situation.

>   A. You try to diffuse the situation. "Wait, wait. Before you say anything, I know I rushed through the data and will look at it again. I'll have it on your desk before I leave today. You are already canceling your much-needed dinner with friends in your head.
>   B. You stand up for yourself and cast blame on others. "Look, I didn't even have to do that stupid report. If other people you

---

[21] Anita Phillips, *The Garden Within: Where the War With Your Emotions Ends & Your Most Powerful Life Begins*, (Nashville, Tennessee, Nelson Books, 2023) XVIII

hired to be on your team would do their job, I wouldn't have to do all the work around here.
C. You crawl under your desk and lay in a fetal position sucking your thumb.

Before you can respond, your boss says, "Thanks so much for the report. I haven't had a chance to read it. My kid fell at soccer practice and broke her arm. I'm on my way to the ER now. I'll try to read it while I'm in the waiting room." Phew! There was no actual conflict- only your perception of potential conflict- but boy, were there lots of feelings bubbling up. It sure felt real!

Conflict rarely happens without emotion. I will go out on a limb and say no conflict happens without emotion. Emotions can move you to hug or hit. The choice, however, is entirely yours. The goal is to recognize and acknowledge our feelings and grow in managing our emotions.

Kendra Cherry summarized the five main purposes of emotions quite succinctly. "Emotions help us to take action, to survive, strike and avoid danger, to make decisions, to understand others. Moreover, they help other people to understand *us*."[22] Emotions are great indicators of what is happening internally. Emotions happen before thought. You don't watch a sad movie and think, "Now I am going to feel sad and cry." How we react in life is filtered first through our emotions. By gaining awareness of our emotions, learning how they are present in our bodies, and understanding their origin, we can move more quickly from emotional reaction to rational thought.

---

[22] Kendra Cherry, "5 Reasons Emotions Are Important," *Very Well Mind*, July 2, 2022, https://www.verywellmind.com/the-purpose-of-emotions-2795181

Name Them and Claim Them

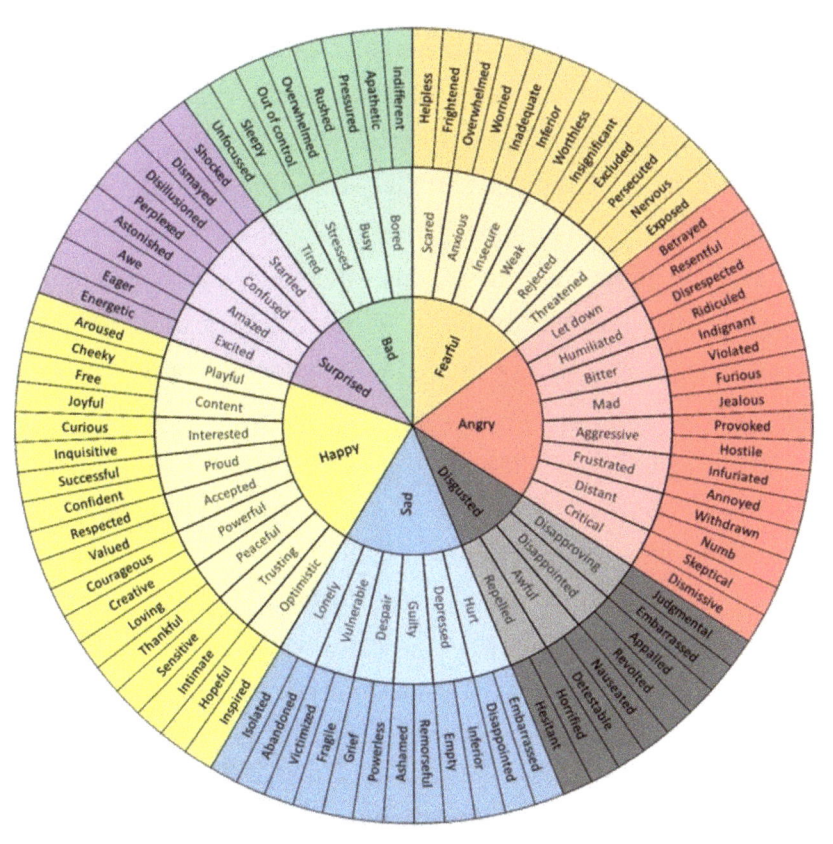

This Photo by Unknown Author is licensed under CC BY-NC-ND

    Above is a diagram of an Emotion Wheel. You will notice that most emotions are ones we might label as negative. They don't make us feel good. I mean, no one wants to experience despair and agony. Please, no! I'll take a double portion of joy and hope with a side of confidence, but all that yucky stuff no thank you. Isn't it interesting that we have more words for negative feelings than positive ones? One reason is that we don't sit and dwell on what we feel in the good times. When I am happy, I don't stop and think about why I'm happy. I'm just happy–Don't ruin the vibe! Those precious times when I'm with someone, and we laugh until we have tears running down our cheeks are levitating. These are the moments that I wish for more of. If I could orchestrate times of joy every day, I would. We would all need less therapy! Unfortunately, these times of bubbling, out-of-control laughter can't really be planned. They just happen. Actually, the more we try to plan joyful experiences, the more we are disappointed, and the experience falls short of our expectations. The big joyful moments of life are fleeting gifts, like when a big gust of wind lifts a kite into the air higher and higher. The very brief, fleeting nature of these moments makes them much more precious. We look up, way, way up! We fly on the wind current of the moment and ride it as long as we can, not daring to look down because we know it will be over soon.

I wish I could experience more of those mountaintop moments with God. Those times He feels so close you can feel His arms wrapped tight around you. I've experienced these moments in worship with others at youth summer camps, sun-burned and giddy with all the passion of young faith. I've experienced these God moments in corporate worship. The times I've raised my voice with hundreds of other voices singing praise songs with every fiber of my being, feeling like Jesus would come through the roof at any moment. And then there are the special, intimate times when I've been alone in the early break of day and heard the inaudible voice of God speaking a message my heart was thirsting to hear.

When we are in these moments that bring about great joy, awe, and wonder, we rarely analyze what we feel and why. We are in the moment. Contrarily, when we are sad, mad, frustrated, challenged, insecure, doubting, or scared, we stop and think, why am I feeling this way? We run to our journals and write down our experiences and responses to situations. We pour out our requests to God. David wrote in the Psalms:

> The righteous cry out, and the LORD hears them; he delivers them from all their troubles.
> The LORD is close to the brokenhearted and saves those who are crushed in spirit. (Psalms 34: 17-18 NIV)

> Is anyone crying for help? God is listening, ready to rescue you. If your heart is broken, you'll find God right there; if you're kicked in the gut, he'll help you catch your breath. (Psalms 34:17-18. Message)

It makes sense then that we have more language to describe the more unwelcomed emotions. After all, we try to understand them because we hope to avoid them. If I analyze why I am sad, I hope I can develop a plan never to feel sad again. Many self-help books are written on the premise that it is always possible to be happy and productive. Even though I wish there were more mountaintop moments in my life, the truth is that God is also in those times we would care not to experience. These times are often when we learn the most about ourselves, God, and others. He is sometimes closest when we feel crushed by life and are most vulnerable. God is in the mundane emotions, the day-in and day-out emotions that come from the monotony of traffic, filing, and yet another load of laundry. Bleh, bleh, bleh. And the truth is that all emotions are a gift from God. No emotion is bad. All emotions happen for a reason.

We are made in the image of God, made by our emotional, heavenly Father. Emotions are God-given, and many scriptures describe our passionate and dynamic God. He is not some aloof, celestial being. He feels love, anger, joy, compassion, and even jealousy.

> For the Lord your God is a consuming fire, a jealous God. (Deuteronomy 4:24)

> For the Lord has comforted his people and will have compassion on his afflicted. (Isaiah 49:13b)

> The wrath of God is being revealed from heaven against all the godlessness and wickedness of people, who suppress the truth by their wickedness, since what may be

> known about God is plain to them, because God has made it plain to them. (Roman 1:18-19)
>
> For God so loved the world that he gave his one and only Son, that whoever believes in him shall not perish but have eternal life. (John 3:16)
>
> Nehemiah said, "Go and enjoy choice food and sweet drinks, and send some to those who have nothing prepared. This day is holy to our Lord. Do not grieve, for the joy of the Lord is your strength." (Nehemiah 8:10)

Emotions have been given to us so that we might not just experience the world through our five senses, sight, smell, sound, touch, and taste, but that we may know and experience life in a profoundly beautiful way. Emotions give us a deep connection to others and to God. How unfulfilling life would be if we couldn't share love. Can you imagine going through life without the ability to laugh? Or cry? Rejoice? Or fight?

Emotions are also for our protection and well-being. They can warn us of danger, like an overflow valve or warning signal indicating we are headed for disaster. They can motivate us and move us to action. Fear can lead us away from situations we need to avoid. Anger at injustice can inspire us to move toward danger.

I've heard emotions described as energy in motion. Emotions can make us do things. Energy has to go somewhere. When we are happy, it bubbles up inside us and comes out as laughter. When we are sad, tears trickle down our cheeks. When we are angry, we raise our voices.

Emotions can motivate us to do the good works we are called to do. Our compassion for others moves us to love in the way Jesus loved. Our hunger for more of God drives us into His Word. Passion and hate of injustice force us to fight for the oppressed.

Emotions can also be very complicated and layered. They can lead us to act or react without thought. They can cloud our vision, making decisions seem murky and confusing. Emotions can birth more emotions, stacking on themselves, creating a knotted mess as seemingly impossible to de-tangle as Christmas tree lights. They can be messy, and they can also be contagious.

An anxious person enters a meeting at work, and the productive discussions turn to worry and become problem-focused. A peaceful evening at home can change on a dime when an angry family member walks through the door. It is easy to spread negative feelings. They can multiply as fast as yeast in warm water. Just a sprinkle of anxiety or anger can change a whole "loaf." Yeast is a small thing, but it works its way through a whole batch of bread dough pretty fast. Just like we learned to wear masks during COVID-19, could we learn to wear a muzzle or duct tape over our mouths when we start spouting angry words? "Post a guard at my mouth, God set a watch at the door of my lips." (Psalm 141:3). Angry words are as contagious as a deadly virus and, some people are more inclined to catch the disease. Some have compromised immune systems, and your little sprinkle of "yeast" or hate may be all they need to send them spiraling downward into despair, or the infection can pass from one person to the next until an entire group of people are infected (1 Corinthians 5:6-8). "He then called the crowd together and said, 'Listen, and take this to heart. It's not what you swallow that pollutes your life, but what you vomit up.'" (Mathew 15:11)

Events can take a downward turn quickly. Stopping a rapidly escalating situation is like trying to stop a freight train. Have you ever attempted to prevent slander and gossip once it gets going? Have you ever walked into the middle of an argument and tried to insert some humor or cheer up a group of people wallowing in self-pity? How did that go? My guess is not very well. Pushing a cart uphill once it has started rolling downward is hard. It can be done, but it requires much more work and effort.

There is No Bear. Just Breathe.

Remember when you were told as a child to "use your words" instead of fists or teeth? This familiar reprimand reminds us to step away from our emotions and think about them. Our awareness of others' emotions and our own is critical in our quest for healthy conflict management.

Emotions are God-given, yet most people are leery or frightened of their emotions. It's as if we don't think our emotions can be trusted. We've experienced emotions out of control in ourselves and others. Emotions can be overwhelming and destructive. No emotion, however, is inherently good or bad. What we do with emotions is what makes them bad or good. It is our response or our actions in conjunction with our emotions that can be negative.

Emotional Intelligence (EI) is the ability to manage both your own emotions and understand the emotions of people around you.

> There are five key elements to EI: self-awareness, self-regulation, motivation, empathy, and social skills. People with high EI can identify how they are feeling, what those feelings mean, and how those emotions impact their behavior and in turn, other people. It's a little harder to "manage" the emotions of other people– you can't control how someone else feels or behaves. But if you can identify the emotions behind their behavior, you'll have a better understanding of where they are coming from and how to best interact with them.[23]

We can't control the emotions of others, but with practice, our own emotions don't have to control us. The hope is that we will gain emotional intelligence so that we can choose what we will say and do despite our emotions. When I become astute at noticing my warning signs and physiological indicators, I can begin to disrupt my habitual patterns. I can have control over my responses in real time.

---

[23] "What is Emotional Intelligence and How Does It Apply to the Workplace," *Mental Health America*, https://mhanational.org/what-emotional-intelligence-and-how-does-it-apply-workplace

Thus when destructive emotions arise – and they will – we can apply our intelligence, educated heart to more effectively deal with emotions in the moment. I want to emphasize it's emotions in the moment that are the issue, because we can learn useful things to do when we're in the heat of the emotion.[24]

No emotion is wrong, but understanding what we are feeling can help us avoid doing something destructive with our emotions. Recognizing our feelings can help us move through life with less friction.

I am no stranger to understanding the complexity of emotions. I have a degree in theatre arts and have been involved in numerous productions on or behind the stage. As an actor, I have recalled and portrayed many emotions on cue. I can read a script and quickly determine a scene's mood, how each character feels, and how their emotions develop as one scene moves into the next. Studying people's behavior has been part of my training in creating believable characters. Art is a reflection of life. I can walk into a room and intuitively pick up on the emotions of others, but ask me how I feel at any given moment in real-time, and I probably can't name the emotion immediately. I have to pause and think to find words to describe my feelings. We rarely take the time to name our emotions. We move through our day, and emotions come and go. We may have had a difficult day full of complicated emotions, but we must keep moving on to the next task, not stopping to process our feelings. It takes intentionality and practice to name and claim your feelings. It's much easier to recognize other's emotions than name our own.

Brene Brown's book, *Atlas of the Heart: Mapping Meaningful Connection and the Language of Human Experience*, the author explores eighty-seven emotions and experiences that define what it means to be human. 87! Can you name 87 emotions?

---

[24] Daniel Goleman, *Destructive Emotions: How Can We Overcome Them?*,(New York, Bantam Dell a Division of Random House, 2003) 259

> Fifteen years ago, when we first introduced a curriculum based on my shame resilience research, we asked participants in the training work-shops to list all of the emotions they could recognize and name as as they were experiencing them. Over the course of five years, we collected these surveys from more than seven thousand people. The average number of emotions named across the surveys was three. The emotions were happy, sad, and angry.[25]

How do emotions play into conflict? We are emotional beings, and conflict is rarely resolved by thought alone, especially if the stakes are high. The role emotions play in opposing forces colliding will be discussed throughout the rest of the book. There are two emotions I want to explore briefly concerning conflict before moving forward. They are anger and anxiety.

<u>Anger</u>

> Sometimes anger can be the highest compliment and the deepest assurance that someone cares for us. This is true especially when the anger directed toward us comes from someone who aims to protect us and make us into the most life-giving versions of ourselves.[26]

Jesus demonstrated that it is possible to get steaming mad and not lose character.

---

[25] Brown, *Atlas of the Heart*, XXi
[26] Sauls, *A Gentle Answer*, 107

> "Sometimes anger, when released from a place of health and love, is a furious force that accomplishes constructive and life-giving outcomes."[27]

I think of Martin Luther King Jr. and many activists motivated by injustice, personal hurt, and deep burning anger, and I thank God for them. But angry people can also wound others and themselves.

> Hurtful behaviors such as violence, scorn, gossip, and slander injure both victims and perpetrators. The hurtful behavior certainly devastates its target, but the hate that lies beneath eats the haters alive, clouding their thinking, crippling their hearts, and diminishing their souls. In the end, those who injure become as miserable as those whom they injure. Those who vandalize someone else's body, spirit, or good name also vandalize themselves.[28]

Anger can be very destructive to all involved. I know what it is to feel angry. I know how my body feels. The term "red hot" comes to mind. My body temperature rises, and my blood pressure increases, which can literally make my face turn red. There is tension in my shoulders, jaws, and chest. Something begins to percolate in my stomach. My arms may fold tight across my body as I try to keep my response to the anger from bursting forth through pointed words and big gestures that may spring out of my body before I can edit them. When I act out of anger, I hurt not only the person on the receiving end of my emotions, but I also hurt myself.

Remember the inciting incident that was described as a flame in Chapter 1? The spark that sets the conflict in motion? Anger can be like fire. Harness it, and it can beat back the cold. Let loose, and it can destroy.

---

[27] Sauls, *A Gentle Answer*, 106

[28] Sauls, *A Gentle Answer*, xvii

When people are angry, they can act in three ways. Picture a liter of soda. The plastic bottle represents the person, and the soda inside is the anger. The bottle is shaken quite vigorously—the pressure mounts inside the bottle. One way to release the pressure is to quickly remove the lid, causing the contents to spew out all over everything and everyone in proximity. Have you ever done the experiment of adding Mentos to a liter of soda? It's kind of like that. The second way to release the pressure is to unscrew the lid gradually, a little at a time. The pressure is released a little at a time through shorts blasts that sound like PPSSSST! Anger can leak out in unexpected ways. The anger may not be targeted so much at the culprit of the anger but at some poor, unsuspecting bystanders. The third way is to recognize and ignore the churning and bubbling inside, hoping it subsides before anyone wants a cup of soda. The person holding onto the anger ultimately feels the effects physically: pent-up tension, stomach troubles, or high blood pressure. Eventually, the pressure builds to the point that the anger can't be contained, and no one wants to be around for that eruption.

The first illustration of the liter of soda is the person who gets angry, and everyone knows it. Their words come out fast and furious without regard for whom the words land on. The person feels a huge relief after the explosion and most likely will leave the situation feeling fine. Everyone else has to clean up the mess left by the person.

The second illustration shows a person who doesn't directly deal with their anger, so it comes out sideways. An example might be someone who is angry at work and doesn't release any of the feelings so that by the time they get home, they are yelling at their kid for not taking the trash to the curb. Then they are frustrated that no one thought to defrost anything for dinner. They throw their keys on the table and slam a few cabinet doors. No one knows what's really going. Not even the person who is in a mood.

The third bottle of soda represents someone who doesn't recognize or deal with their anger. They pretend nothing is wrong, and they really might think nothing is wrong. The anger will settle down, but over time, a person may be sitting on so much pent-up anger that it comes out in a huge explosion, scaring everyone around them, including themselves.

Anger is complicated. It is not what I would call a "stand-alone emotion." Brene Brown discusses this in Atlas of the Heart. There is an ongoing debate about whether anger is a primary or secondary emotion. Brene concludes, "The more data collected…the more certain I became that anger is a secondary or "indicator" emotion that can mask or make us unaware of other feelings that are out of reach in terms of language, or that are more difficult to talk about than anger."[29]

Becca Stevens, president of Thistle Farms, shares how women process anger after unthinkable abuse. Thistle Farms has, for 25 years, lit a pathway of healing and hope for female survivors of trafficking, prostitution, and addiction. Becca tells stories of women "who thank their rapists for driving them back into town instead of leaving them on some remote roadside."

> Months later, the rage they should have directed at their attacker emerges and turns small issues into huge arguments. They are finally and rightfully angry as hell. Anger can feel like an explosion that can destroy relationships and community. But, seriously, anger is just the surface stuff. There is so much underneath it, and if you can find a way together to get to that, it is powerful and life-changing. Remember that the next time you want to blow! What the hell is underneath this powerful feeling? And the next time someone yells at you, for just the next breath, stop and remember; this is where the deep soil lives."[30]

---

[29] Brown, *Atlas of the Heart*, 221
[30] Becca Stevens, *Practically Divine*, (Harper Horizon, 2021) 99

<u>Anxiety</u>

When I was going through my journey of depression, someone told me about a book entitled, *Feeling Good: The New Mood Therapy*, by David Burns.[31] This book contains an exercise that I still do regularly. I rarely have to write anything down on paper now, but I used to practice this exercise in great detail when I first started implementing it into my life. I can typically now do the exercise in my head. The exercise is this: You divide a piece of paper into two columns. In the left column, you write a thought without editing it. What is the thought or feeling you can't seem to shake? That thing that is stressing you or causing lots of feelings. Write it all out. Then read what you've written. Underline the parts of what you wrote that are factual. You know it to be 100% true. Cross out what you now see may not be accurate, and your initial perception of a situation may have been incorrect. Then, re-write the same thoughts/feelings with edits. Here is an example:

---

[31] David D. Burns, MD, *Feeling Good: The New Mood Therapy*, (New York, William Morrow, 1999)

The Story I'm Telling Myself	**Facts**
My friend didn't invite me to go to dinner with her and another mutual friend. When I asked her to dinner last week, she said she didn't have time to go out to dinner, but here she is going out with someone else. I think she doesn't want to be around me anymore because I annoy her or she's mad at me. Maybe she's jealous of my new position. She always excludes me. I never get to spend time with her one on one. She must like this other friend better than me. I need to stop talking to her about my job. I am burdening her too much with my problems. I'll just stop sharing any of my stuff and focus more on her. Or maybe I should just ghost her like she has me.	I wasn't invited to dinner. She is out to dinner with another friend. She often invites me to things. We had quality one-on-one time last month. Conclusion: I am hurt because I wasn't invited this time, but I have been invited many times before. My friend can have (and should have) more than one friend. These two may need to discuss something alone.

So much of what we dwell on isn't reality. I have read Philippians 4:6 as a command not to be anxious, that anxiety is a sin. That's not what the verse implies at all. "Do not be anxious about anything, but in every situation, by prayer and petition, with thanksgiving, present your requests to God" (Philippians 4:6). The verse says to examine your thoughts and feelings, but don't stop there. Pray about them. Reflect on them and talk to God about them. It also implies that anxiety is a recurring emotion. It's not something we take to God, and it never occurs again. The verse says, "In every situation," being anxious is a part of the human condition. I did a quick Google search to see how many Bible verses there are about worry or anxiety. This is not a scholarly search by any means, but Google cites between 50 – 60 verses about worry and anxiety. This doesn't even delve into the verses dealing with fear, which is a first cousin of anxiety. Much like anger, anxiety can be a complex emotion. If you are anxious, what is causing the anxiety?

The danger with anxiety is that it can often cause us to enter a fight that's not based on reality but on imaginary issues or problems. There is a lot of energy behind anxiety. It manifests in the body, and the message from the brain is, "Something has to be done right now!" But is doing something or nothing the best course of action? Referring back to the situation in the columns above: How might the next conversation between the two friends have gone had the person not taken time to get to the bottom of her initial interpretation of her friend's lack of invitation to dinner? Would it have been a good encounter? We can quickly begin to spin into playing out worse-case scenarios. What happens when we act while we are stuck in a spin cycle? What if the friend who felt slighted had confronted her friend telling her their friendship was over because she always felt excluded? How unfortunate it would be if a relationship ended based on an assumption that had spiraled out of control. If you often feel anxious, I highly recommend the above exercise. It will help quiet your racing thoughts so that you can think more productively.

> A genuine reflective life engages practices that allow us to slow down and listen. When we do this, the Spirit helps us see our automatic, habitual ways of responding when anxiety shows up in our relationships.[32]

Anxiety also breeds anxiety. Just like anger, anxiety can be very contagious. Again, anxiety is an emotion with lots of energy behind it. When someone is highly anxious, everyone around them knows it.

---

[32] Herrington, *The Leader's Journey*, 9

When anxiety rises, we become rather predictable. Our thinking becomes less clear and more reactive. Some of us withdraw; others engage in conflict. We begin to place or accept blame in an effort to avoid taking responsibility for making personal changes. We begin to see ourselves as the victim of other's actions. We assign motive to other's behaviors, or we take it personally. Demand for conformity in thinking and behavior increases. We look for a quick fix to symptoms that develop.[33]

Brene Brown suggests that anxiety leads to two forms of coping: worry or avoidance. She concludes "…worry is not a helpful coping mechanism, that we absolutely can learn how to control it, and that rather than suppressing worry, we need to dig into and address the emotion driving the thinking."[34]

Don't stuff the anxiety. Dig it out and bring it into the light. This is the way to stop what can be the spinning cycle of anxiety. If anxiety is controlling you more than you are controlling it, it may be time to talk with someone about things that can help with anxiety. Talk therapy, tapping, or medication are common practices in helping to manage anxiety. There are many more tools that can help in the managing of anxiety. Friend, you do not have to live with an anxious heart! As I mentioned, I used medication and therapy to help with my depression. I shudder to think what my life would be like had I not taken bold steps to get help.

This awareness of our emotions is so important in handling conflict well. We don't want our words, actions, or responses to be born from unresolved feelings. We need to dig up our stuff and deal with it, if we are going to be our most whole and effective selves, especially in times of inevitable friction.

---

[33] Herrington, *The Leader's Journey*, 31

[34] Brown, *Atlas of the Heart*, 11

Our garden's foundation is looking better and better as we rid ourselves of unwanted debris. The soil is healthier and ready for planting. Before we begin to choose what we want to grow in our lives, we need to protect all the work we have done. We need good fences!

Reflection/Discussion Questions:

- Take a few minutes to look over the Emotion Wheel. Which emotions do you often experience? Which emotions do you often encounter in others? Which emotions seem unfamiliar or foreign to you? Look at how the wheel is organized. Is this how you would organize emotions? What do you notice about the subtle differences between the emotions in each category?
- As you look at the Feeling Wheel, notice what specific emotions you associate with conflict. Write them down. What do you notice about the emotions that you named? How does your approach to conflict relate to your experience with these emotions?
- Try the exercise that Kristy described. Divide a piece of paper into two columns. In the left column, write about something that has happened without editing it. Include the situation as well as your thoughts and feelings and assumptions about it. Now re-read it and underline the things you wrote that are knowingly and factually true. Lightly cross out everything else. On the right side, write the story again, this time based in reality. Notice the difference between the two stories and wonder about how the story you are telling affects how you experience life.

Chapter 5

Building Fences

>...Before I built a wall I'd ask to know
> What I was walling in or walling out,
> And to whom I was like to give offense....
> He says again, 'Good fences make good neighbors.'
> "Mending Wall" by Robert Frost

IF YOU HAVEN'T figured it out by now, I love plants. It is almost an obsession with me. When I go to SeaWorld, and everyone is in awe of the Beluga Whales or the King Penguins, I will take detours and marvel at the landscapes. They are magnificent. As I look at plants of various colors, shapes, and sizes, a few statues and waterfalls cascading here and there, I will turn to David and say, "This is how I want my backyard to look." Alas, I do not have a team of gardeners or unlimited funds to maintain such beauty, but I enjoy my small attempts at gardening.

In the Texas hill country, I've learned that I can't plant something based on its beauty or even how I know trailing vines would look perfect spilled over a specific rock. Oh no. Before ever falling in love with any foliage, I must see the words "deer resistant" written on the pot. I have learned the hard way that deer can be pests.

One morning many years ago, I awoke early to the smell of coffee and the sun slowly waking up the world. Bible study in one hand and coffee in the other, clad in my robe and slippers, I stepped out onto our deck only to find that deer had delicately nibbled off the flower heads of almost every plant. My deck, once clothed in color, was now naked. The deer, those magnificent creatures, were bold enough to invite themselves for a late-night snack. And so, I look for "deer resistant" when purchasing plants.

Armadillos are also a nemesis for Texas lawns. After falling in too many holes dug by armadillos and having too many plants munched on by deer, we finally built a much-needed fence to keep critters out and plants safe. The fence was the boundary I needed to create, cultivate, and tend my garden. It was necessary and made my work so much easier. Sure, some other pests and diseases could not be kept at bay by installing the fence, but I no longer worried about the things I knew could not get through the boundary we purposefully built.

Boundaries are dividing lines. They separate one space from another, creating a clear line of where the garden begins and ends. If you don't have some border around your flower beds, you will have unwanted weeds slowly creep in and take over the bed. If you are not careful, the weeds can choke out what you intentionally plant. The unwanted vegetation slowly invades the space, gradually over time. Eventually, the landscape will look nothing like what you had dreamed or hoped. Clear boundaries are one of the first lines of defense in keeping our lives on track.

So, what kind of border or boundary do you need to protect your garden? You've worked hard at clearing land and designing your ideal space, so what do you require to keep it growing and flourishing? Are you more of an open country split rail fence kind of girl, or is a red brick solid enclosure more your style? What kind of barrier do you need to keep yourself healthy and thriving? Like me, you might think you'd like to have a specific fence because it sounds good and seems more socially acceptable. Again, let me encourage you not to compare yourself to others. Consider what you need to stay mentally, physically, and emotionally healthy, not what someone else needs, wants, or expects from you.

I know people who seem to always have a clean house and an open-door policy for everyone. They love having people in their homes. The more people, the better. They have numerous friends, are involved in many activities, and are constantly giving back to the community, AND they always seem happy and content. I would love to live like this, always available to everyone with a jam-packed calendar of activities. I did live like this at one point in my life and ended up in the pit of depression because I was not living the way God created me to be. I am more of a Zen/country garden. I have to have alone time to stay balanced and mentally healthy. I require solitude to recharge. I need a slower, contemplative life, but I also need purpose and activity. I know this about myself and try to create an environment where I can thrive best. One of the best ways I can manage my mental and emotional health is by creating appropriate boundaries.

I don't live isolated, but I don't have an open-door policy. People are invited into my space. In the garden of me, I have a clear dividing line that makes it clear to all that they have to go through the gate to get to me. Think of it this way: if you were out for a walk and a neighbor was in their yard, and you called out to them and said hello, and they waved back, would you walk up to their fence, open the gate, and go in? No. You might walk up to the gate and start talking over the fence, but you wouldn't go inside unless invited. There is a boundary there for a reason.

What kind of fence would you have to keep your garden thriving? Not the kind of fence you wish you had, but the one you need. What kind of gate would be best for you? Perhaps you have a modern clear glass enclosure with a gate that resembles a turnstile. Maybe you have a white picket fence with a gate that has an easy latch to open. Perhaps a red brick, six-foot-tall structure with a keyless entry is more your style. There is also the option of barbed wire, cattle guard, and a cumbersome gate with chain and padlock. Are any of these boundaries wrong? Ugly? Not appropriate? We will talk more about boundaries elsewhere, but for now let me say this: your boundaries are created by you. They are yours to design. They are there to keep you safe and sane. Is there anything wrong with that? I don't think so.

Nedra Glover Tawab has done a lot of work in the area of boundaries. I love to hear her talk. She has a Southern drawl that can be soothing as she verbally smacks you upside the head. I have laughed out loud while listening to her on various podcasts more than once. Nedra writes that unhealthy boundaries lead to burnout, resentment, frustration, superhero syndrome, anxiety, and depression.[35] How do boundaries help us when engaging in conflict? What happens if you are burned out, resentful, frustrated, anxious, or depressed and you are faced with a challenging situation or conversation? What happens when we enter a conflict while the light on our giving tank is flashing red, warning of imminent and inevitable depletion? I can tell you if I'm hungry and someone crosses me, chances are our exchange is not going to go well.

The superhero syndrome Nedra speaks of is the unreasonable belief that they [you] can do everything, often without the support of others. How do you think a difficult conversation is going to go if you feel indestructible or superior? My guess is not very well. The other danger of superhero capes we often wear is that we take on more than we should, which leads us to more burnout, resentment, frustration, anxiety, and depression.

Without healthy boundaries, we can get overwhelmed, and our capacity to add one more thing to our lives is gone. Our generous souls are depleted as we watch things begin to fall off our proverbial plates. Our capacity for compassion for ourselves and others is diminished. "Compassion is the daily practice of recognizing and accepting our shared humanity so that we treat ourselves and others with loving-kindness, and we take action in the face of suffering."[36] According

---

[35] Nedra Glover Tawwab, *The Set Boundaries Workbook: Practical Exercises for Understanding Your Needs and Setting Healthy Limits*, (New York, Penguin Random House, 2021) 10

[36] Brown, *Atlas of the Heart*, 110

to Webster's dictionary, compassion fatigue is "apathy or indifference toward the suffering of others as the result of overexposure to tragic news stories and images and the subsequent appeals for assistance."[37]

I think the world was suffering from compassion fatigue in 2020. I know America was. Everyone was dealing with too much. It was all just too much: a global pandemic, racial tensions, political unrest, and no united answer to anything. Not only were we bombarded with all the bad going on around us via social media and endless news cycles, but we each were facing our own challenges: illness, unemployment, supply shortages, isolation, working from home, and homeschooling for the first time.

I thought the common threat of a pandemic would bring out the best in Americans much like it did with the bombing of the World Trade Center in 9/11. It didn't. It brought out the worst. People were afraid. Everyone was afraid. We were like animals backed into a corner, ready to protect our own. People were panic buying, hoarding what each thought they needed. Stores had to limit the number of items people could purchase, especially toilet paper. The hoarding of toilet paper will go down in history as a strange COVID phenomenon. What was the obsession with toilet paper? There was little compassion for the next guy as we greedily grabbed what we needed, real or imagined. We all felt threatened by some unseen enemy. It turns out it is hard to come together when separated by six feet, masks, and partitions. We had a common enemy, a virus, but we did not have common answers on the best way to deal with it.

More than a sad commentary on the state of our nation, what we experienced was a glimpse into our humanness. America was not as invulnerable as we thought. We had limits. It turns out we weren't "invincible with liberty and justice for all." We were just as fragile as other nations, nations we had pridefully thought inferior to us; we were flailing in the fight of a deadly virus just like everyone else. We

---

[37] Merriam Webster Dictionary, "compassion," Accessed January 25, 2024, https://www.merriam-webster.com/dictionary/compassion

universally had compassion fatigue. We could not help each other because all our resources were being used to care for our own. There was nothing left to give to others. The impact of this depletion of compassion resulted in conflicts between family members, church members, colleagues, and friends. It was no longer clear who was for us or against us.

Compassion fatigue occurs when our nervous systems are overwhelmed. Living from crisis to crisis can make us numb or indifferent to what is happening around us. When I think of examples of compassion fatigue, I think about watching shoot 'em up movies with my husband. Now, the truth is, I like action movies. I am never forced to watch them; however, I do like it when the dialogue is at least as lengthy as the fight scenes. I do want a plot and some character development. Sadly, this is not always the case. When watching a movie with too many intense car chases and crashes, or when the villain rises from the dead for the third time, I find myself stifling the desire to scream, "Oh come on! Die already!!" I have reached my limit of compassion for anyone. I just want it to be over.

We certainly don't want to go through life in a place of apathy–when we don't or can't care anymore. I think apathy may be the greatest sign of mental distress. There's nothing left for us to give because we have either been de-sensitized or depleted. But how do we keep our compassion levels up? Brene Brown writes about compassion in *The Gifts of Imperfection*. She explains that the way to replenish our capacity of approaching others with loving-kindness is through implementing boundaries. When I read that boundaries were needed in order to be compassionate, I was like, "Wait. What?" I thought compassion meant you gave, gave, gave, and boundaries meant you said no, no, no. How can the two be connected? How can building a fence make me more compassionate toward others?

> Well, it's difficult to accept people when they are hurting or taking advantage of us or walking all over us. This

research has taught me that if we really want to practice compassion, we have to start setting boundaries and holding people accountable for their behavior....
When we fail to set boundaries and hold people accountable, we feel used and mistreated...It also impossible to practice compassion from a place of resentment. If we're going to practice acceptance and compassion, we need to start by setting boundaries and accountability.[38]

I recently heard a friend longingly say all he wanted to be able to do was to take a nap, and I thought, well, you can. What's stopping him from taking a nap? Isn't it interesting how we think we can't do the things we long to do? Or the things we know our bodies need us to do? We say things like, "I wish I could be the one who sits in worship service and doesn't serve anywhere." Or "I wish I could eat a whole cheesecake." Or "I wish I could take time off to do whatever I wanted." Or "I wish I could Fill In the Blank." Guess what? You're not in jail. You can do what you want, need, or desire. Your boundaries are not a prison. In fact, they are there to help you live a more abundant life.

The Set Boundaries Workbook lists "Seven Benefits of Setting Healthy Boundaries:"

1. You'll reduce any feelings of guilt.
2. You'll rid yourself of some unhealthy relationships
3. Your healthy relationships will improve.
4. You'll discover your strength.
5. You'll create relationships that make you feel happy.
6. You'll learn to respect other people's boundaries.
7. You'll improve your ability to be assertive in multiple areas.[39]

---

[38] Brown, *The Gifts of Imperfection*, 26-28
[39] Tawwab, *The Set Boundaries Workbook*, 14

I find #6 intriguing. It is interesting that the more we are aware of our own boundaries the more respectful we are of the boundaries of others. We recognize the right of others to protect themselves from an often intrusive and difficult world. It is easier to understand the "no's" of others as their rightful decision instead of rejection. As carefully as you have planned and prepared your garden, hopefully, they have carefully and purposefully planned theirs. Just like you would never want someone else to come into your space uninvited and start pulling up weeds, you should never go into someone else's space with a lovely rose bush and start digging a hole because you know that is just what they need.

I have found #7 to be true. Boundaries will improve your ability to be assertive in multiple areas. If I have a clear idea of who I am and what is most important to me, I then have a better idea of where and when to assert myself. I know where I start and you begin. I am more sure of what is rightfully mine to do.

Boundaries will come up more as we get into specific conflicts, but remember that you don't want people in your garden uninvited. So, you can't go in theirs. They've worked as hard as you on their garden. That is their space. Only Jesus gets to move fences and re-arrange plants, and even He will not do it without permission. You worry about yourself. It's not your responsibility or right to beautify the rest of the world on your terms.

Reflection/Discussion Questions:

- For a day or two, use your phone to take photos of the various kinds of boundaries you see in your daily life. How many examples of boundaries can you find? How effective are they? Where are there missing boundaries? What is the result?
- As you consider the garden of your life, what does it need protection from? What predators or pests invade your space and ruin your plants? Once you know what your boundaries are

protecting you from, you can begin to design the boundaries that are right for you. Do you need a quaint garden gate or a brick wall? Barbed wire or a pretty border? Use your imagination to picture what your current boundaries are like as well as what you would rather put in place.

- Look around your life for Nedra Glover Tawab's list of symptoms: burnout, resentment, frustration, superhero syndrome, anxiety, and depression. If you see one or more of these, check the nearby boundaries. Are they missing or broken? Take them one at a time and consider how you might restore them.
- What is the connection between compassion and boundaries in your life? Do they rise and fall together, or have they become separated from each other? Do you tend to think of compassion as positive and boundaries as negative? How could boundaries and compassion work together in your life?
- When have you said wistfully or resentfully, "I wish I could . . . (fill in the blank). Say it out loud so that you can hear it. Now, without changing what is in the blank, make a tiny change: "I wish I *would* . . ." Does anything shift for you, even slightly? What possibilities can you see?

Chapter 6

The Line That Will Not Be Crossed

Our worth and belonging are not negotiated with other people. We carry those inside our hearts and I'm not going to negotiate that with you. I may fit in for you, but I no longer belong to myself. – Brene Brown

IN 2022, MY parents passed away 11 months apart. They were married for 67 years. They say that couples who have been married that long will rarely live past a year after the other spouse dies. My dad lived shy of a year after his beloved wife left this earth. My sister and I did our best to see them the long way home. Theirs was a long, hard end. Weeks after my father's burial, it was time to decide on a headstone, so I reached out to the person at the funeral home who designed the headstones. Over a few days, we emailed a few ideas back and forth. One afternoon, I heard the familiar ping of my computer and opened my email. I saw these words and dates:

James L. Carson	Robbie L. Carson
11-18-29	4-4-34
4-18-22	5-28-21

I stared at the screen dumbfounded. These were just letters and numbers supposedly summing up my parents' lives – simple dates to sum up two complex people and their lives. Was that it? Their whole lives, and that was it? A granite plaque grave marker? The cemetery didn't even allow headstones. All that could memorialize them was a rectangular stone on the ground where a few words were written. The marker also included some beautiful roses and a cross, which, for some reason, was oddly comforting to me. At least it wasn't just their names and dates. All their striving, giving, and sacrifice culminated in these few words? Poof. It was over. That's all there was? The futility of life engulfed me like a black rain cloud. It hung heavy over me for quite a while. Their grave marker was a stark representation of their lives. It also represented a huge personal loss for me. Grief hit me hard. I was faced with the reality of life ending. Their lives ending – just gone – empty – no more. A whole generation of saints was leaving this earth. I missed them. I still had so many questions I wanted to ask. Who else would ask me about every doctor's appointment? Who else would know I even had an appointment? Who else would talk to my sister if she drove at night to ensure she got home and inside safely? Who else would tell me they were so proud of me? Profound loss.

I was also faced with this reality: I am now the matriarch. The generation in front of me, gone. Not to be morbid or pessimistic, but realistically, I feel my days are numbered. I am pondering more and more what I want these last chapters of life to be.

There is a poem that is commonly used at funerals. As I looked at the dates on my parent's grave marker, from birth to death, I thought of this stanza.

The Dash Poem by Linda Ellis

So, when your eulogy is being read
With your life's actions to rehash...
Would you be proud of the things they say
About how you spent YOUR dash?[40]

---

[40] Linda Ellis, "The Dash," https://lindaellis.life/the-dash-poem

The Line That Will Not Be Crossed

I began to ask myself some hard questions. What do I want people to say about me after I'm gone? What do I want to accomplish before I leave this earth? All of this pondering resulted in some short-term and long-range goals. In retrospect, my existential crisis was very beneficial and fulfilling; however, as I looked forward, I needed to look back. Sometimes, the clearest way to see in front of you is to look behind you. You need to be careful about living in the past, but there are great lessons to gain from reflecting on your life thus far. What parts of my past served me, and what parts did I need to change? As I examined my behavior during the past five years, I recognized many times when I acted out of character or behaved in a way that I would describe as not typical. Considering my personal struggles, it was not surprising that they affected every area of my life. However, there were broader reasons for my behavior changes.

We have experienced so much upheaval and difficulties as a nation in the last few years it is understandable that we are a little off-centered, not entirely ourselves. A global pandemic, political polarization, social unrest, and increased violence are just some of what we have had to face. Church denominations are splitting and dividing. There is so much division that it's hard to know what topics are safe to bring up in casual social settings. It is no wonder that I respond in inconsistent ways. We are living in turbulent, confusing, and inconsistent times.

During this national unrest, I cared for my elderly parents and a sick grandchild. I worked when I could and, quite honestly, was doing more surviving than thriving. Life can be as amazing as it is awful, and I had lived on a rocking, free-falling, and heart-stopping roller coaster for far too long. My nervous system was shot, and surprisingly, the world does not stop simply because you need a moment to catch your breath. I was pitched and thrown like a bull rider at the San Antonio rodeo. I rode that out-of-control ride until I didn't recognize myself. I had lost perspective in my dizzy life. It is hard to find your way when spinning from one crisis to the next. Once my parents died and my granddaughter was healthy and home, I caught my breath for the first time in years. I mean for the first time I was able to really take a deep breath and lower my shoulders from my ears. I looked around and thought, "Now what?" I had spent so long reacting to immediate needs that I didn't know what to do.

I realized I had lost myself once again. Yes, again. Finding oneself is an ongoing process. I remember having the same sense of not knowing who I was when I had small children. Those times when I felt like I was meeting myself coming and going when my greatest accomplishment for the day was to shower and get dressed. Sometimes, the best we can do is hold on and ride the ride. Some seasons will demand more of us than we think we have to give. Other times will allow us more space for reflection and re-grounding.

After giving myself much grace over my somewhat murky identity, I made a pact with myself to take the time to define who I was, who I wanted to be, and how I wanted to be known. What did I want my dash to be?

Many years ago, I had a theatre professor who gave an assignment for every script we were assigned to read. The assignment was very simple but very difficult. We were to read a full-length play and finish this sentence in one word: "This play is about _____." ONE word! I hated this assignment. I felt like I could never get it right. I would sweat over my reply. I can vividly remember the small class sitting in a circle and each student having to share their answer. We would go around the circle and say things like love, family, connection, or relationships. My teacher would look at us like we were clueless, which we kind of were, and say with great confidence, "No! This play is about regret!" She would then fill a huge whiteboard spanning the length of one wall in the classroom with evidence of her theory. She would map out how every character, word, and punctuation pointed to regret. As they say, "we were schooled." I hated this exercise because it was hard, but guess what I do today before I direct a play? I write on the first page of the script, "This play is about _____." I usually end up more with phrases like, "This play is about lost opportunity and hope for redemption."

That doesn't fulfill the requirements of the original assignment, but it helps me see and focus on the overarching meaning of the play. This exercise is like drawing a plumb or chalk line when building a house: A straight line is drawn on the foundation of a building, and everything built refers back to this line. It keeps the house straight and solid. If your measurements do not refer back to this initial and critical marker, your house will start to lean or worse, collapse.

What is the plumb line of my life? My inner world can be very squirrel-ish. Very. I have a racing mind full of random thoughts all of the time. I needed something to focus me. Something that would always be available to me. I set out to distill my life into one sentence, one word. I know I am more than this, but I needed something clear and simple to keep me anchored in the storms of life. How would I finish this sentence, "My life is about _____?

I was reminded of a hymn I have sung many times, mainly in a Baptist church with a robe-clad choir and organ pipes blaring. It was often one of those songs that could be heard from the church parking lot. Edward Mote wrote these words in 1834.

> My hope is built on nothing less
> Than Jesus' blood and righteousness
> I dare not trust the sweetest frame
> But wholly lean on Jesus' name
> On Christ the solid rock I stand
> All other ground is sinking sand
> All other ground is sinking sand

The teachings and truth of Jesus are my foundation. When the stormy gales rage, He is to whom I turn. The church is "built on the foundation of the apostles and prophets, with Christ Jesus himself as the chief cornerstone."(Ephesians 2:19-22)

Historically, the cornerstone was the most important part of any building. The total weight of an edifice rested on this particular stone, which, if removed, would collapse the whole structure. The cornerstone was also the key to keeping the walls straight. The builders would take sightings along the edges of this part of the building. If the cornerstone was set properly, the stonemasons could be assured that all the other corners of the building would also be at the appropriate angles. Thus, the cornerstone became a symbol for that which held life together.[41]

I can come up with a list of things I can do to embody the life of Jesus, but the assignment given to me by my professor wasn't to come up with a character analysis but the theme of the whole work. I started focusing not on what Jesus did but on why and how He did it what He did. Remember those WWJD (What Would Jesus Do) bracelets? Maybe we need new ones that say WWJDT, Why Would Jesus Do That? Who Jesus was determined what He did – and why.

In *The Garden Within*, Dr. Anita Phillips shares a story about a friend who was given a dog. This friend traveled for work and knew she would be away from home more than was needed to care for a young puppy. Her friend was faced with a difficult dilemma. What to do with this animal?

So what to do? The thinking began.
Can I return the puppy to the breeder it was purchased from?
Do I personally know anyone who wants a dog?
Might the dog sitter adopt him?
My friend's thinking did *not* include questions like these:

---

[41] "Building on the Cornerstone," *Back to the Bible,* January 23, 2019, https://www.backtothebible.org/post/building-on-the-cornerstone

The Line That Will Not Be Crossed

How far into the Arizona desert do I need to drive to abandon the dog without being seen?
Shall I take the dog to the parking lot at the grocery store and offer it to strangers until someone says yes?
Those thoughts never crossed her mind. Why not? They were outside her belief system. Those thoughts could never sprout from seed of beliefs in her heart.[42]

The equation I used to find my one word went something like this behavior + motivation = my value(s), in that order. I was choosing what words defined me most by what I did. In looking at the previous dog story, my values and beliefs are the roots from which my motivations and behaviors come – my values are my plumbline. The equation actually looks like this: Values + Beliefs = Motivations and Behaviors. What values do I want to filter my life though? What one or two words do I want to be the line that I go back to, the line that keeps all of my actions and behaviors centered in the way I desire? If I were a person who would ever get a tattoo, this word or words would be written on the inside of my arm so that whenever I get tired, over-whelmed, or face a giant, I could look down and be reminded of who I am.

The Fruit of the Spirit is an excellent place to start.: Paul writes in Galatians 5: 22-23, "the fruit of the Spirit is love, joy, peace, forbearance, kindness, goodness, faithfulness, gentleness and self-control." The beatitudes also have some good ones: meek, merciful, peacemaker.

When push comes to shove, who do you want to be? We must be clear with ourselves about what we believe and hold to be most important. What we believe and hold most important will decide our values and belief system. Our actions, responses, words, thoughts, intentions, decisions, and behaviors align with those values and beliefs. It is very helpful to distill my values and beliefs into just a few words.

---

[42] Phillips, *The Garden Within*, 123

I could use many words, but I want something quickly available to remind me who I am.

And so, I will give you the assignment my professor gave me many years ago. Fill in this blank, "I want my life to always be about _____." Your word(s) are yours. You may have a word that means something to you that no one else would understand. Here is a list of words to get you started, but the choices are endless.

List of Values and Beliefs

Accountability, Adaptability, Adventure, Altruism, Authenticity, Balance, Beauty, Compassion, Curiosity, Creativity, Contentment, Excellence, Energy, Fairness, Faithfulness, Freedom, Friendship, Fun, Forgiveness, Generosity, Grace, Gratefulness, Humility, Honesty, Hope, Integrity, Insight, Independence, Joy, Justice, Kindness, Loyalty, Love, Leading, Maturity, Organization, Open-mindedness, Patience, Playfulness, Peace, Pride, Rest, Righteousness, Reliability, Security, Spirituality, Success, Thankfulness, Vulnerability, Whole-heartedness, Work, Wisdom.

****

After you choose your word or words, let me suggest telling people you know. Gulp. Does that make you nervous? Are those the words they would have chosen for you? Do friends and family see you living out those words every day? How about strangers and enemies? How about when you feel threatened or confronted? Are these words that would describe you when engaged in a stressful situation?

This exercise could quickly be like many of our New Year's resolutions. We are committed to them on the 31st of December but by

The Line That Will Not Be Crossed

January 15th we are trying to remember what we vowed to change. Life's demands can so quickly engulf our best intentions.

I recently was able to access my value words in real time in a stressful situation. I was meeting a friend at Cava. Cava is a restaurant where you stand in line and tell the people behind the counter what you want in your bowl, salad, or whatever. It was particularly crowded on this day. I arrived before my friend but got in line, knowing she was right behind me. There were at least 15 people in front of me, and quickly, a line was forming behind me. All of the tables except one were taken with people who had obviously left the line and were saving the table for their party. My friend and I had not seen each other in months. The whole point of our meeting was catching up on each other's lives. I was beginning to wonder if we'd even get a table. As many others had done, I decided to leave the line and sit at the only available table. I sat down and took out my phone to let my friend know I was saving a table when I heard a rather loud voice say, "Don't sit down." A lady I did not know was looking directly at me and talking to me from across the restaurant. Half of the place had to have been able to hear her. She proceeded to instruct me not to sit down and save a table because when all the people got their food, there would be nowhere for them to sit. This lady is drilling a hole through me with her laser-focused eyes. She is looking only at me. Her stern demand was directed right at me. I could feel the heat rising to my face as I'm sure many people were looking at me, waiting for my response. My adrenaline kicked in.

My body reacted as if it was under attack, and let me tell you, it felt like I was under attack. In that split second, before some reaction was necessary, all of the research to write this book came back to me. The match had been struck and a flame was burning. Conflict was inevitable, but I had a choice in how I would respond. I began to practice what I've learned. I looked down at my forearm and saw my imaginary tattoo. In my mind's eye I saw *integrity* and *kindness* written on my arm *in black ink and scrolled font*. Integrity means lots of different things to me, but it especially means that I will be the same person at the grocery store as I am when I teach kids at church on Sunday mornings. At that moment, I knew how I would respond. I had planned it long before the lady spoke to me.

Did I leave you hanging? Want to know what I said? Before I share my response, how would you have responded? What would you have said? What would you have done? This experience was so good for me as I got to pull apart and analyze the whole situation. Was this lady right to call me out in public? Was I wrong to sit down? How could I handle the situation better next time? What responses could I have ready should I find myself in a similar situation? I even asked other people what they would have done. They had some great ideas. I learned so much from this chance encounter!

When we find ourselves in an embarrassing or difficult situation, we can be so thankful that the whole ordeal/conflict is over that we run from the experience and ignore what we can learn from it. Maybe we share the incident with others, but seeing the conflict as an opportunity for growth is so important. I want to learn from confrontational moments. I want to prepare myself for the inevitable conflicts of life. There is always room for improvement.

Just FYI – everyone I have asked about the lady's aggressive request to not sit at the table thought this lady was incredibly rude and out of line to call me out like that, but you know what? Even though it took a while for my body to come down and re-calibrate after the encounter, I was proud of how I handled the situation. I didn't cower but didn't engage or escalate the situation. I smiled at the woman and said that I was waiting on my friend and we would decide what we were going to do. It could have gone in a very different direction. I'm learning. It is a work in progress for sure, but I am learning.

Like my Cava interaction, there are many battles we find ourselves in that are not of our choosing. Can we be better prepared for these unexpected encounters? After reading, studying, and searching, I can say with great confidence, sort of, maybe. The answer is both yes and no. You can determine your reactions up to a point, but our innate defense mechanisms are strong and kick-in reflexively. The next three chapters will dive into the wonders of our FFFF responses.

Reflection/Discussion Questions:

- Kristy shares a poem about our life's "dash." What would you like people to remember most about you?
- Have you experienced a time(s) in life when you felt you had lost your identity? When was it, and what have you done since then to rediscover it? Did you come out the same as before, or entirely different?
- Kristy shares a few lines from a song and verses in the Bible that are meaningful to her when she considers her life's purpose. What is the foundation or cornerstone of your life? What do you feel is your purpose on this earth?
- What are your top two value or belief words? Why are these so important to you? Do you feel like you are currently living in alignment with what you value most? If not, how can you move towards that?
- Kristy describes an incident at Cava where she dealt with a difficult conflict. Do you feel Kristy acted in line with her values? How would you have responded?

Chapter 7

The Reactions We Do Not Choose: The FFFF Responses

Lions, and tigers, and bears, oh, my! Lions, and tigers, and bears, oh, my! Lions, and tigers, and bears, oh, my!

-The Wizard of Oz

There was a situation at work. I found myself in the middle of two strong forces with no good way out. I was pressed by the person in charge of me and getting pushback from the people I was trying to lead, "trying" being the operative word. Everyone had an obvious agenda and no one was going to like how this was going to end. I was caught between a rock and a hard place. I felt cornered and these opposing forces were closing in. I wanted to be loyal to all parties, but there was no way to make this a win/win situation.

I came home after a particularly stressful day full of hard conversations. No one was happy, especially not me. My home phone rang. (This was years before cell phones.) I tentatively checked the caller ID. It was indeed someone from work, but it was a friend who was thankfully not directly involved in the work situation. I answered the phone relieved to have a friend who I thought was considerate to call and check on me during this difficult time…ummmmm…bestowing kindness upon me was not her intention, however.

I don't remember exactly what this person said to me during the phone conversation, but it was a brutal and personal attack on my character and ability to lead well. I remember hanging up the phone and sobbing. I felt like a complete and utter failure. Moments later, I experienced my first full-blown panic attack. I wasn't sure what was happening. I thought I was having a heart attack. Logically, I knew I wasn't in any physical danger, but it felt like it. Eventually, I was able to take deep breaths and produce some logical thought.

Confused, battered, and bruised, I called a wonderful friend. I chose this friend because she did not live near me and had no connection to my work or its people. I also called her because she was a therapist and would keep our conversation confidential. I asked her if she could recommend a counselor in my area because I was obviously broken and needed help. She asked me a few questions, and in the course of just a few minutes, this trained and gracious friend said four words that I still cling to today. She told me, "There is no bear."

"There is no bear" is what I've learned to say to my body when I need to calm and center myself. When I feel overwhelmed, stressed, or threatened, saying these four words have become a mantra I repeat to myself until I feel I can have more control of my emotions and actions. My dear friend helped me understand that when I felt under attack my body responded like a bear was chasing me. My body didn't know the difference between imminent physical danger and a verbal altercation. The body's responses were the same for both. My body was literally ready to flee and get me to safety. My heart was pumping, and my muscles were prepared to RUN! But I didn't run because no bear, lion, or tiger (Oh my!) existed! I didn't move, and so I was left with a rapid heartbeat, tense muscles, increased adrenaline, and no knowledge of what was happening to me. Hence, I felt like I was having a heart attack.

My friend explained that our bodies and brains' primary function is to keep us safe. When we were hunters and gatherers and were out in the woods and encountered a bear, our bodies would instinctively respond to the danger, so our bodies did what was needed to

The Reactions We Do Not Choose: The FFFF Responses

protect us. However, the reality is that we rarely encounter wild animals in modern civilization, disgruntled and angry people, perhaps, but not typically bears. This was my first introduction to the Fight, Flight, Freeze responses.

F^3, or the Fight-Flight-Freeze response, is the body's automatic, built-in system to protect us from threats or danger. For example, when you hear the words, "Look out!" you may be surprised to find how fast you move, and thankfully so, as you narrowly miss a flying baseball sailing through your kitchen window! Or when you see a bear on the trail up ahead, you freeze and remain quiet until it moves on. In both scenarios, your system effectively protects you from danger.

> The F^3 system is critical to survival from actual threat or danger, but what happens when there is no real danger? Interestingly, our perception of danger can also trigger this system into action when we believe there is a threat, even if there is not. "For example, you may yell at your partner for pushing you into agreeing to speak at a conference when you don't feel ready (fight). Or you avoid going to a party or leave early because you don't feel comfortable around unfamiliar people (flight). Or, your mind goes blank when your boss asks you a question (freeze). All of these are examples that can cause anxiety, which, in turn, can mistakenly trigger the F^3 alarm. Public speaking, parties, and answering questions are not dangerous situations, but if your alarm system is set to "high alert" it will go off even in relatively harmless situations."[43]

God has beautifully wired us so that we can protect ourselves. Our bodies contain an amazing innate function, the unconscious and

---

[43] "Fight-Flight-Freeze," *Anxiety Canada*, *https://www.anxietycanada.com/articles/fight-flight-freeze/*

automatic recognition of threat and danger. When we perceive imminent danger, our bodies respond as if walking through the woods and encountering a giant bear. Our instincts kick in, signaling we must do what is needed to survive. Our choices are that we can fight, freeze, or flee. We can stay and fight for our lives. We can flee to escape the danger or freeze, hoping the threat will pass without our involvement. Our sympathetic nervous system drives these responses. Fight, flight, or freeze phenomenon is primitive and hard-wired into our DNA. The prefrontal cortex automatically goes offline, and our brain's reptilian or instinctual part takes over to protect us. There is no thought before action. There is just a reaction. Sometimes, the physical overwhelms the brain's capacity to function logically. These are not the fights we choose. You don't go looking for these encounters. They find you, but the reality of the danger feels so real and so strong they are impossible to ignore.

The title of this chapter, *FFFF Responses*, alludes to a fourth F. Indeed, when fighting, fleeing, or freezing is not the best choice to protect ourselves, we may call upon the (F)awn response. "The fawn response is when an individual tries to avoid or minimize distress or danger by pleasing and appeasing the threat. Someone responding in this way would do whatever they can to keep the threat, or abuser, happy despite their own needs and wants."[44]

We Aren't So Different from Our Furry Friends

We, like all mammals, have an amazingly protective nervous system. The following stories may remind you of watching a series of cat reels on TikTok, but I find the study of animal behavior helpful in understanding human responses to stress. Unlike humans, language or social conventions do not limit or alter animals' primal and instinctual

---

[44] Katy Kandaris-Weiner, LPC, "What is the Fawning Trauma Response?" *Inner Balance,* (July 26, 2023) https://innerbalanceaz.com/blog/what-is-the-fawning-trauma-response#:~:text=The%20fawn%20response%20is%20when,their%20own%20needs%20and%20wants.

behavior. It is what it is, in its purest form. Humans have this same primitive response to danger as animals. We may be more capable of hiding or covering our reactions to fit social norms, but the body's reactions are the same.

Fawn Response

We currently have two dogs. One is a tiny little chihuahua mix named Zeke. The other is a medium size fluffy mutt, Charlie. Charlie is at least three times the size of Zeke and three times his age; however, Zeke is the dominant dog. An Alpha male is the animal that is more dominant than the other animals in a pack. Zeke is the alpha male of the two dogs. Not only does he get first dibs on special treats and available laps, but he also sits on Charlie. Yep. Poor Charlie lays down, and Zeke plops his butt on him. It doesn't look comfortable for either, but there's no doubt who is in charge.

I have also seen cats put large dogs in their place with one growl or claw to the nose. It is clear to animals who has the power. There may be a struggle, but it becomes clear in the end to all who is in charge. One dominates, and the other acquiesces to the powerful one. A hierarchy is established to minimize fights and physical harm until the dominant animal is challenged, and the cycle repeats.

An example of the fawn response is seen when two animals face-off against each other and one suddenly rolls over onto their back. The one who is on his back playfully bats the other animal with its paws and no longer appears aggressive. The submissive animal now seems innocent and docile. It is behavior meant to let their opponent know that they mean no harm. Suddenly, like a flipped switch, they are no longer confronting but placating as if to say, "Who me? I would never fight you."

Fight Response

    We had a dachshund, Sam, who suffered from little big-man syndrome big-time, often overcompensating for his stocky, little legs. Once, he tried to take down a full-grown man who came into our backyard unannounced. Picture a grown man being pushed backward by the bark and sheer fierceness of a six-inch tall dog. Sam has taken on huge German Shepherds, killed rabbits three times his size, and once tried to attack a 2000-pound bull. I didn't say he was smart, but he is fierce. An animal will protect itself, its territory, and its loved ones.

    Watch a mother protect her young if you want to experience a full-out, aggressive example of the innate nervous system. We have barn swallows in Texas. Once these birds have built a nest and had babies in a location, they will return to the same place and even the same nest year after year. Unfortunately, we have a family of swallows that chose our front porch. As adorable as it is to watch these baby birds hatch, grow, and fly every year, I'm not too fond of the mess they leave. I've tried all the tricks recommended to get them to move locations: painted the ceiling blue, hung fake snacks, bought fake owls, used sound machines, and came out each dawn in my pajamas swinging a broom over my head. None of these things deterred the swallows, and I have given up. Not only do these birds make a mess, but they also protect the eggs and babies fiercely. After I had hosted a lovely dinner, a swarm of swallows chased my guests to their cars as they left. These tiny birds banded together to protect the next generation.

    Have you ever seen a group of placid cows with big brown eyes? What harm could they do? Come between a mother cow and her calf; she will plow you over. If she senses you are a threat, sweet Bessie will stomp you into the ground. She WILL fight. Gone are her memories of the special molasses you put in her feeding trough. The seemingly docile and slow-moving cow will take you out. Ask any Texas rancher. Respect the Mamas. Give them a wide berth. It is also best if you don't walk behind a horse unannounced. If the horse cannot see you, the horse may think you mean him harm, and he will kick you. Hard. Like brain-dead hard.

Animals will fight if they or their loved ones are threatened, even when the odds seem stacked against them. There is no thought to personal danger. There is no future thinking or planning. An innate survival instinct kicks in and takes over.

Freeze Response

Have you ever encountered a cat or dog fight and interrupted their circling and howling? Inevitably, one animal will freeze, and the other will run off, thankful for the opportunity to run to safety. Opossums freeze to the point that they play dead. When threatened, opossums go limp and fall, eyes open and glassy, and their tongues hanging to the side of their mouth, appearing dead. The opossum has little or no control over when this happens. It is a literal default function of their little opossum body. It's hardwired into their nervous system. The dachshund mentioned above once treed an opossum in the back of our property. The poor opossum instinctively froze and fell out of the tree. From all appearances, the animal was dead. Our dog barked, sniffed, and pushed the opossum around until he knew he was dead, and then the dog sat back on point, guarding his trophy. Feeling no longer threatened, the opossum would come to life and start to move. The dog would attack, and the opossum would fall dead. This song and dance continued until I went out and picked up the brave dachshund and carried all 10 pounds of him inside the house.

My grandfather loved to tell a story about a cat and a rattlesnake. My grandparents lived next door to us—a well-worn path created mainly by a beloved granddaughter lay between our houses. Our family had a fluffy yellow cat named Sunshine. Behind our two houses were open fields where Sunshine was prone to explore. One day, my grandfather stepped onto his back porch and heard the distinct, high-pitched sound of a rattlesnake's tail. The snake was just beyond my grandparent's backyard. Sunshine and the rattlesnake were staring each other down, frozen except for a rapidly moving rattle.

At this point in the story, my grandfather would get very intense, describing how no muscle, not one eyelash, twitched on either animal; apparently, the snake was a girl with long lashes. The telling goes that the rattlesnake was giant, and his size grew with each telling. In our family, the only good rattlesnake is a dead one. My grandfather moved as quickly as possible to get his shotgun. He finally dug the gun out from the back of the closet, fumbling to get it loaded, but by that time, he was out of breath, and his heart was racing. He had to sit down and let one of his nitroglycerin tablets melt on his tongue. Finally, he made his way out on the back porch, thinking he surely had missed his opportunity to kill the snake, but Sunshine and the snake had not moved. My grandfather moved closer and closer until he was able to get a sure shot. Once the snake was dead, he says Sunshine fell to the ground, so weak he couldn't move. The cat used every ounce of energy, keeping his body rigid and frozen. His total focus was on the danger in front of him. The rest of the world faded as he chose the best means to avoid the snake's bite – freeze.

Flee Response

Walking through a forest, you can hear various animals scurrying to safety. I have laughed myself silly watching videos of animals being startled. My still traumatized husband tells the story of entering his third-floor apartment as a medical student, startling his friend's cat he was "cat-sitting," who was perched on the balcony railing. Without thought, the cat startled, falling off the rail and onto concrete three floors below. David ran to the railing and looked down, afraid of what he might see. The cat was shaking off the fall three floors below. Apparently, cats really do have nine lives. No cats were harmed in the telling of this story!

The Reactions We Do Not Choose: The FFFF Responses

The Two-Legged Animals

These are cute animal stories, but what about humans? With all of our deductive reasoning and the use of language we possess, do we ever react without thinking? No thought at all before reaction? Surely, we have evolved and are above all this primal reaction stuff, right? Do we really exhibit the same fight, flight, freeze, or fawn defenses? You betcha. It is a part of the internal warning system in each of us. Like all animals, and yes, we are animals, our brains' and bodies' primary purpose is our survival. In the next chapter, I share examples of human behavior under threat and stress. Remember, we have the same primal protective system as our fury friends, which, to summarize, involves an involuntary moment of basically losing it, coming undone, having a hissy-fit, or flipping our lid!

If you are like me, it is mortifying to think that I will be so out of control that I can't predict my responses once my FFFF responses kick in. Here is the good news: all the work we have done thus far can help us in the moment when we recognize we feel threatened or afraid, and there is still more to learn about preemptively determining how we respond when we "flip our lids."

Self-reflection is an important part of understanding how you respond in conflict and how to do better moving forward. When confronted with a conflict (willing or unwillingly), do you tend to fight, freeze, flee, or fawn?

Reflection and Discussion Questions:

- Kristy recalls a time when she was caught in the middle of a situation at work. A friend confronted her and made pointed verbal attacks. How do you feel when confronted by someone?
- Describe a time when you had to deal with a difficult conflict. Did you fight, flight, freeze, or fawn? Are there ways you would've handled this differently now looking back?

- In most conflicts we encounter, there really is no actual bear. How can this knowledge help you the next time you are in a challenging conflict?
- Even if there is no actual bear, our brains still experience the phenomenon of "flipping our lid" when we feel threatened or scared. What are some coping strategies you use that can help calm your brain and nervous system?

Chapter 8

<u>Flipping Your Lid</u>

The Sky is Falling! The Sky is Falling! – *Chicken Little*

"FLIPPING YOUR LID" is an idiom that refers to when our thinking brain goes offline and we react instinctually. There is no time for thought. Our reactions are fast and unpredictable. We've all experienced it. While driving, someone in another car does something that startles or scares you. Their driving skills may evoke a swerve, honk, or hand gesture. In your "right mind," you would never act this way. As your nervous system calms down, you pray that the person you just emphatically waved at isn't someone you know. What caused this uncharacteristic behavior? These responses occur when the lower parts of our brain take over, and our cortical or thinking brain becomes disconnected.

The following hand diagram is an excellent illustration of "lid flipping." Dr. Daniel Siegel, a clinical professor of psychiatry and author of *The Whole-Brain Child and Mindsight: The New Science of Personal Transformation,* came up with a simple way of explaining the concepts of fight, freeze, and flight.[45] The hand model of the brain is a helpful way of showing the brain's functions and what happens when we "flip our lids." The thumb represents the limbic portion of our brain. "The limbic system is the part of the brain involved in our behavioral and emotional responses, especially when it comes to behaviors we need

---

[45] "Our Reaction to Stress Explained: How to use 'The Hand Model of the Brain,'" *Building Better Brains: Together We can,* (December 24, 2019)

for survival: feeding, reproduction, and caring for our young, and fight or flight responses. You can find the structures of the limbic system buried deep within the brain, underneath the cerebral cortex and above the brainstem."[46] The four fingers in the diagram represent our brain's thinking and reasoning parts, the prefrontal cortex. When threatened, the limbic part of our brain takes over. It is reactive. Our thinking goes momentarily offline. This instinct is shown by the four fingers "flipping" up and the thumb region of the brain taking over.

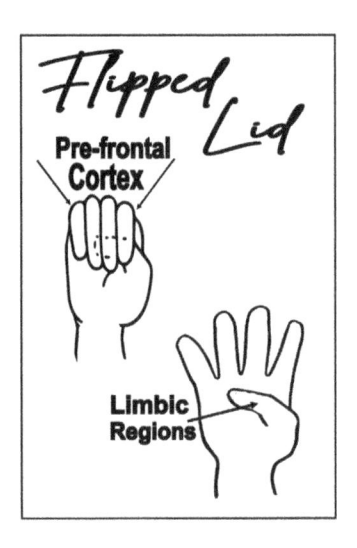

Flipped Lid

Pre-frontal Cortex

Limbic Regions

When we have 'flipped our lids,' the different parts of our brain are not integrated, and as such, we cannot learn, communicate our needs, stay connected with others, or problem-solve. In this state, it is difficult, if not impossible, to handle conflict calmly or rationally. We are in a reactive state. Our bodies and brains protect us. Our brain's primary function is to keep us alive.

---

[46] "The Limbic System," *The University of Queensland, Australia*, https://qbi.uq.edu.au/brain/brain-anatomy/limbic-system#:~:text=The%20limbic%20system%20is%20the,and%20fight%20or%20flight%20responses.

Flipping Your Lid

Lid Flipping in Action

In the last chapter, we saw how animals experience and demonstrate the four FFFF responses to threat. Their primal instincts take over, and their bodies and brains work in tandem to do what they do best – protect and survive! We may watch cute animal videos for a good laugh, but the truth is that God has instilled within us an unfathomable ability to withstand great stress and threats. It is remarkable how efficient and miraculous our bodies are. Instead of cringing at all those embarrassing moments when I jumped or screamed as someone unexpectedly came around the corner, or the time I convinced my family I smelled smoke and made them all leave the house, knowing it was on fire (FYI – it wasn't), or the time someone honked at me in a parking lot, so sure of my rightness that I circled around to confront them…..wait….okay…really that is still embarrassing, but the point is this: We.Are.Remarkably.And.Wonderfully.Made.For.Survival! Let's take a moment and marvel at how our Creator knew we would need survival instincts. Like our furry friends, we respond in much the same way to danger, real or imagined. The following are examples of the human FFFF responses in action.

Fight Response

One night, as my husband was in a deep sleep, he was awakened by a crazy woman sitting in the bed next to him screaming at the top of her lungs, "There's someone in the room! There's someone in the room!" The crazy woman was me, and I had had a nightmare. My husband's survival instinct kicked in, and he bravely flung a pillow with great force into our pitch-black bedroom, aiming at an imagined enemy. This action made me love this man even more for his willingness to be my brave protector, wielding his soft and squishy pillow, clad in his Fruit of the Looms armor. Bless him—poor man. I, of course, had no recollection of the dream or the scream and turned over and went back to sleep. He, however, laid awake with eyes wide open, staring into the darkness, willing his heart rate to slow down for a good long while.

The pillow-tossing story is a funny illustration of our fight instinct and an excellent example of how quickly we respond to threats. No thought, just action. Bless him!

This is a humorous story of the fight response, but it is this very response that allows people to run into burning buildings to save someone. Or fight an attacker against all odds. The fight response sends our bodies into overdrive, and we feel we can accomplish super-human tasks. When I was in college, my roommate and I were walking back from the library when someone came beside me and snatched my purse. Without thought, I screamed and started running after him. My roommate threw down her books and joined in on the chase. Some guy we didn't even know riding on a moped saw the whole thing and started jumping curbs and riding cross-country to catch up to the purse snatcher.

The whole time the three of us were in pursuit, we screamed for the thief to stop. We caused such a ruckus that we caught the attention of the campus police. Two policemen joined the chase. The combined effort of two college girls on foot, a guy on a moped, and two police officers in a car, culminated in the tackle of the thief. I'm unsure who got to him first, but I think it was the brave moped boy. As I finally caught up to the scene breathless and with a twisted ankle, I saw a large man on the ground in handcuffs, fighting the policeman who had his knee in the man's back. The policeman had to use his body weight to keep the thief down on the ground. It finally hit me that I had been in a dangerous situation. In the moment, I wasn't afraid at all. I was mad. I felt violated. No thought. Just action. If you had asked me before this incident how I would have responded to someone taking my purse, I would have never said I would have chased the guy across campus until I got my purse back. Never. But that's what I did.

What would I have done if no one had helped me catch the guy? I shudder to think how the incident might have ended. Not my wisest decision, but that's the point, isn't it? There was no decision—just action.

That day, I learned a vital lesson: Determining or controlling how we respond in certain situations can be difficult. I also learned to be more compassionate when others react in ways that don't make logical sense. We will all have those moments when we flip our lids – and there isn't any logic to our responses.

Flee Response

I went to the zoo with my daughter and her three young children. We were at the lion exhibit, where a large, healthy male lion walked close to the glass enclosure. I was enthralled and thrilled that the children could see this magnificent creature so close when the lion suddenly lurched toward us and roared. I took off in the opposite direction so fast that I stumbled over a baby stroller in my escape route. That stroller held my precious grandbaby! Forget the children! I am going to be eaten! Oh my!! There was no thought for anyone or anything. My instinct was to run! I've always told my children I would take a bullet for them. I would jump in front of a moving train to protect them. When told on airplanes to put my oxygen mask on first before placing it over my child's mouth, I always thought, "no way, the kid comes first." Apparently, my kids do come first, except when a lion is involved. My flight response was alive and well.

It is fascinating that before my brain could even process the word danger, my body responded to protect me. Have you ever felt the hairs on the back of your neck stand up before your mind acknowledged what caused the phenomenon? Have you known in your gut something was off and wasn't quite right before you could logically assess a situation? Your body gives you vital information all day long. Listen to it. Pay attention to the messages. Your body's primary function is to keep you alive and safe.

Freeze Response

When I think of the freeze response, I think of the scene in Jurassic Park when the little girl knows a T-Rex is behind her. The terror in her face is palpable. You can feel the energy radiating from her. Her body is operating in overdrive, ready for action, yet she is frozen because moving is not a safe option.

Have you ever been alone in your house and heard a noise? One of the funniest experiences with freezing happened when we lived in Colorado. David and I were in bed late at night. We had turned out the light when we heard a sound in the kitchen. Our dishwasher had started! We heard our dishwasher turn on. We froze. We didn't breathe and could barely speak. Who started the dishwasher? Now we laugh thinking about it. Was someone breaking into our house to wash dishes? How dare they! We will never know what happened, but I will tell you it took a lot of courage to walk into the kitchen that night to check out the notorious Cleaning Burglar!

The freeze response is also a gracious gift at times. It is documented that people only retain 40%–80% of information shared by medical personnel, and the percentage goes down based on the seriousness of the illness.[47] I have witnessed the freeze response in hospital rooms when loved ones receive bad news. Facial expressions go blank. Shoulders droop. Responses slow. The information is too much for the nervous system. There's nothing to fight and nowhere to flee where the news will not follow. The body's innate need to protect itself graciously kicks in, and everything slows down until the mind can process and accept the medical report.

---

[47] Roy P.C. Kessels, Phd, "Patients' memory for medical information," *Journal of the Royal Society of Medicine*, (May 2003), https://pubmed.ncbi.nlm.nih.gov/

Flipping Your Lid

Fawn Response

When fighting, fleeing, or freezing aren't the best choices for survival, just like animals, we may call upon the fawn response. In a nutshell, fawning is using people pleasing to diffuse conflict, feel more secure in relationships, and earn the approval of others. This is often seen in movies when a person in power, such as a president, CEO, or celebrity, takes advantage of a mild-mannered assistant, friend, or relative who tells them what they want to hear or does whatever the person in power demands. The audience cringes as the person in charge walks over the submissive person.

One summer, my husband, daughters, and I were on a family mission trip to Vermont. Everyone on the trip took a needed work break and walked down a single-lane, picturesque road. We were crossing an old bridge, pausing for picture opportunities, when a truck, blaring loud music, barreled down the hill and across the bridge. Thankfully, everyone had quick reflexes and jumped out of the way. No one was hurt, but the truck sped on without stopping. Several people yelled things like, "watch out, slow down!" The truck squealed to a stop and started backing up as fast as it had been going forward. Some of us had to jump into a ravine to avoid the backing truck. The driver and his passenger glared at us, barking, "What did you say?" These two men were looking for a fight. They wanted to fight someone. Two shotguns hung from a gunrack behind their heads. Thankfully, one of the couples with us stepped up and waved. The husband took his wife's hand. They both said very calmly, "Nothing. We didn't say anything. Hope you enjoy your day. We are just out for a walk." As they spoke, we followed their example, started slowly and calmly gathering children, and continued to walk in the opposite direction, showing the people in the truck that we didn't want a fight. Any other response to this threat could have ended badly. In the animal world, we did the equivalent of rolling over on our backs and making ourselves very small. We were physically communicating that they were the alpha males and were happy to let them keep that title.

Your own experiences may have come to mind as I shared my memories of acute stress and feeling threatened, and I'm sure we could share funny, scary, and even tragic stories for many hours. You may be embarrassed by some of your reactions under extreme stress. You may wish you had handled certain situations better. I certainly feel that way, but I am beginning to understand how quickly my brain strategizes how to protect me best. When you "flip your lid," all logical thinking goes out of your ears. You are in survival mode. Understanding my nervous system's responses to danger helps me have grace for myself and extend grace to others. Our brains are doing the best they can with the available information. Instead of erasing these embarrassing or frightening moments from my mind, I am choosing to thank God that my brain can protect me so quickly even when I am unaware it is happening. That is amazing.

We all possess this innate need to protect ourselves. If someone is afraid or feels threatened in any way, they will react. The Bible records people responding under extreme stress. People with the best intentions and motives respond surprisingly as their body's primary function kicks in to save and protect. What can we learn from reading their stories?

Biblical Examples of FFFF

In the garden of Gethsemane, some of Jesus' disciples found themselves in a life-threatening situation. Unknown to them, the they had shared their last supper with Jesus. Judas had already left the group to fulfill his predicted betrayal of Jesus. The 11 followed Jesus to the Garden of Gethsemane. Once in the garden, Jesus said to the disciples, "sit here while I pray....My soul is overwhelmed with sorrow to the point of death...stay here and keep watch." (Mark 14: 32–33) Jesus' confession of His troubled state is so touching. He is vulnerable and hurting. He needs their protection and prayerful intervention on His behalf. Jesus specifically asks them to do two things: stay awake and pray. Peter, James, and John stay closer to Jesus than the rest. Jesus went ahead of them "a stone's throw away" to pray. (Luke 22:41) Jesus asks Peter, James, and John three times to stay awake and pray.

The Message Bible describes the event so well:

> He (Jesus) came back and found them sound asleep. He said to Peter, "Simon, you went to sleep on me? Can't you stick it out stick it out with me a single hour? Stay alert, be in prayer, so you don't enter the danger zone without knowing it. Don't be naive. Part of you is eager, ready for anything in God, but another part is lazy as an old dog sleeping by the fire. He then went back and prayed the same prayer. Returning, he again found them sound asleep. They couldn't keep their eyes open, and they didn't have a plausible excuse. He came back a third time and said, "Are you going to sleep all night? No–you've slept long enough. Time's up." (Mark 14:43-47, MSG)

All 11 men were too tired to keep their eyes open. None had heeded Jesus' warnings of what was to come: betrayal, denial, and His death. They hadn't noticed the signs, the rising tensions, nor the heaviness of their Master's heart. They were not ready for what was to come or obedient to what He asked them to do, "stay awake and pray." Instead, they were at their most vulnerable: asleep and defenseless.

The 11 are startled awake by the sound of a "gang of ruffians" (Mark 14:43 MSG), a "crowd armed with swords and clubs" (Mark 14:43 NIV). Ten of the disciples freeze at the sight of "swords and clubs" and "an angry mob." Startled awake, Peter's instinct is to fight. He grabs a sword, swings, strikes a high priest servant, and cuts off his ear. Then, the 11 disciples flee, one leaving behind his clothes. "A young man, wearing nothing but a linen garment, was following Jesus. When they seized him [Jesus], he fled naked, leaving his garment behind." (Mark 14:51 NIV). I have two responses that immediately enter my mind. The first is condemnation for their behavior of abandoning Jesus. My second follows almost immediately. How very human of them. Would I have responded any differently? Their survival instinct is strong: to fight and then flee.

Peter's memorable denial of Jesus as a rooster crows shows a man desperately trying to make sense of an unfolding nightmare. His life and the life of his beloved leader changed in a moment.

> Meanwhile, Peter was in the courtyard below. One of the servant girls who worked for the high priest came by and noticed Peter warming himself at the fire. She looked at him closely and said, 'You were one of those with Jesus of Nazareth.' But Peter denied it. 'I don't know what you're talking about,' he said, and he went out into the entryway. Just then, a rooster crowed. When the servant girl saw him standing there, she began telling the others, 'This man is definitely one of them!' But Peter denied it again. Some bystanders later confronted Peter and said, 'You must be one of them, because you are a Galilean.' Peter swore, 'A curse on me if I'm lying—I don't know this man you're talking about!' And immediately, the rooster crowed the second time. Suddenly, Jesus' words flashed through Peter's mind: 'Before the rooster crows twice, you will deny three times that you even know me.' And he broke down and wept. (Mark 14:66-72)

Peter exhibits the fawn response as he feigns ignorance of the whole situation. He denies he was a follower of Jesus. And finally, he emphatically denies knowing Jesus at all. This scene makes me cringe. I can see Peter cornered. I can feel his fear. His eyes are darting around, looking for a way out. He tries to make himself small and invisible. He tries to hide in the shadows and lose himself in the crowd, but people keep drawing the focus back to him. He doesn't resemble the loud, brash, gregarious Peter we've experienced in the rest of the Bible. He is protecting himself in any way possible.

I have heard people discuss how they would have reacted, if they had been the followers of Christ in the garden that night. I don't know if anyone knows how they would have responded, but I think we all can relate to feelings of shame and regret over our blunders and missed opportunities. Thankfully, few have had their embarrassing moments historically documented for all eternity. I have several thoughts as I re-read this passage. The first is how Peter could deny knowing Jesus three separate times. One time, ok, I get it. Two times, maybe. But three times?! How would I have responded if my life was in danger for simply knowing someone? Would I have bravely stood beside Him and helped carry His cross?

Jesus knew of Peter's denial before it happened. He knew none of His disciples were going to stay with Him. Jesus knew that wasn't the way it was supposed to play out. He told Peter he would deny knowing Him three times before the rooster crowed. Jesus knew Peter. And Jesus knows us. We are messy, complicated humans. We make mistakes, big and small. How do you respond when you are faced with your humanness? How would you react, if your cowardice and humanness were brought to light? How would you respond to protect yourself?

I've been there. Have you? Cornered with no way out. A finger pointed at you. Eyes drilling holes in you. Accusations hurled at you.

- "Did you copy his answers?"
- "Did you take credit for her work?"
- "Did you lie?"
- "Did you fail the test again?"
- "Were you the one who told the boss?"
- "Did you tell her the thing I told you in private?"
- "Did you spend all the money?

- "Did you take it without asking?"
- "Were you drunk when you were driving?"
- "Did I see you with another man besides your husband?"

How do you respond? Do you fight the accuser? "How dare you accuse me of such a thing! You're one to talk!!" Do you freeze, willing a hole to swallow you up? Do you flee, saying over your shoulder, "Can't talk now...." Or do you respond as Peter did? "What? I don't know what you're talking about. Who told you that? You must have seen someone else."

I hurt for Peter. I can imagine the shame he felt. He did the very thing he promised not to do. The irony is that the man Peter denied knowing is the one who will, just hours after the denial occurs take Peter's shame to the cross and, in doing so, offer him forgiveness forever. And He offers the same to you and me.

So, what do we do when we have flipped our lids? When we have taken our sword and struck before knowing the whole picture? When we are fleeing away from danger, feeling so vulnerable, we may as well be naked running in the woods. Are there ways to help close our lids, or are we truly left defenseless? Are we prisoners to these inevitable paralysis moments of irrational thought? Again, I will answer yes and no.

We can't predict when we will face situations that will flip our lids, but we can prepare ourselves for those inciting incidents that lead to rising tensions. We can also understand triggers and body cues that can give us some control during these high-stress moments. We can make some preparations for the unexpected battles we will face. An excellent place to start is to learn from our past FFFF experiences.

Reflection and Discussion Questions:

- While "flipping our lid" can help explain our behavior, it is not an excuse for us to treat others poorly. How do you maintain (or regain) control when you feel lost in the moment?

- What might happen if you interact with others instinctively and not in accordance with your true values and feelings? How might you handle or repair a situation after you have flipped your lid?
- Often, we discuss responding according to fight, flight, freeze, or fawn in a negative way. As Kristy notes, survival instincts can provide valuable information. Why are these responses important? How can you use this information? Has there been a time when your FFFF responses have warned you of significant and real danger?
- Kristy gives us multiple examples throughout the chapter of how responding out of instinct can lead to embarrassment and shame. Have you ever experienced this? Have you been surprised by the ways you've responded to situations? If so, how easy is it for you to extend grace to yourself for these reactions?
- Kristy discusses how even Peter from the Bible betrayed Jesus. She discusses feeling torn between condemnation and compassion for him. What do you think about this? How does understanding the FFFF responses help us understand and have compassion for others?

Chapter 9

<u>Flipped Lid</u>

> My soul has a bad habit of magnifying what isn't so good and godly. Too often I focus my inner magnifying glass on the nasty comment some stranger made, and it grows…Or I put it on the future, and the endless stream of fear, anxiety, and worry expands into a river that sweeps me away.[48]

WHAT CAN WE gain by revisiting our past FFFF moments? We may never want to think about those times because no one likes to be out of control or look like a fool. We all have those times when we flipped our lids in less-than-elegant ways. We also may find that revisiting past FFFF moments stirs up unpleasant memories. For some, living in crisis was a way of life. The dangers endured were not imagined but very real.

As children, we develop coping skills for navigating the complexities of life. Our young minds have strong memories that shape who we are and how we perceive the world. We adapt to our surroundings to create safe and secure environments. I know some had childhoods that were never safe. Living from crisis to crisis was or is a way of life for some. Others have survived unspeakable trauma, and for this, I am so very sorry. There is so much good work happening now in the area of trauma. Trained professionals can help to unearth past events in such

---

[48] Brett, *Be the Miracle*, 25

a way that healing can begin. Please allow me to encourage you to find a qualified professional to help you on the healing journey. You don't have to be a prisoner of your past.

Our bodies remember trauma. We carry strong memories into our everyday lives that have dug trenches of neuro pathways in our brains. We will continue to respond the way we have in the past because that is what our brain knows; that is what we did to keep ourselves safe as children. As adults, those patterns of behavior may no longer be serving us. It may be time to respond to acute stress differently.

Then there are those times when we are not in real danger, and there really isn't a bear, but we still have to deal with our innate warning system. Those FFFF responses can be over the top for what situations warrant. We can create new neuro-pathways, if we want more control over our responses. Our brains are malleable! It turns out you really can teach an old dog a new trick!

Speaking of dogs, I again find evidence of human behavior by observing our dog. Please indulge me yet again as I share another animal story. We have a dog named Charlie. We got Charlie from an animal shelter. He was cute, fluffy, and very friendly but never truly calm. He only relaxed when he was sound asleep, and often, his sleep was disrupted by nightmares. It didn't take long for us to realize he was abused at some point. If you raised your arm and he was nearby, he would cower. We would never have hit him. Our arm raising could have been to scratch our head or reach for something. We tried daily to make Charlie feel safe, but he was always alert for physical punishment. It took years for Charlie to trust us. We had Charlie for probably two years before he stopped flinching when we moved suddenly. It was closer to ten years before he would relax against us and snuggle. He still has nightmares, but he no longer fears us when he is awake. Through time and experience, Charlie's sympathetic system re-adjusted. Charlie learned we did not mean him harm. We were not a threat.

With time and intention, we can change our patterns of behavior, even our instinctual patterns. It is not a quick fix or an overnight cure, but it is possible.

I think back to the disciples in the Garden of Gethsemane. Peter fought while the remaining eleven disciples fled. Later, Peter fled but was unable to abandon Jesus completely. I picture Peter hiding in the shadows and trying to overhear conversations, hoping for information about where they had taken Jesus. He heard where they had taken his teacher and went to find him. Perhaps Peter thought he could stand strong and stand by his friend no matter the consequences. He desperately wanted to do the right thing, but when the time came, he could not rally the courage. He betrayed his friend by denying Him three times, but that is not how the story ended. The disciples' story did not end with the horrific garden scene. Thankfully, we have the rest of the story.

The disciples each became strong advocates for Jesus, many to the point of death. They suffered greatly for their faith and often met violent deaths because of their bold witness and faith in Christ. Peter, who denied knowing Christ three times, was martyred in Rome around 66 AD. He was crucified upside down at his request since he did not feel worthy to die in the same manner as his Lord. How did this change come about in these men's lives?

I'm sure these men had all the emotions we have when facing perceived danger. They weren't miraculously immune to pain, suffering, or fear. At some point, they not only claimed to have known Jesus, but they boldly proclaimed Him as their Lord and Savior. They were bold as they delivered their messages to governments and kingdoms that Jesus was the one and only true King. The disciples' new bravery was evident and hard-won. They stood on a foundation of knowing that it may be scary and dangerous, but in the end, it would all be worth it. They were human. They knew fear. But they knew they didn't want to run or make excuses when it mattered most. Don't you know that when a lie or the desire to appease started bubbling up in Peter, he quickly squelched it, saying to himself, "No way. Never again."

Observing yourself under stress can help determine how you will respond in the future under extreme pressure. If we revisit how we reacted while experiencing the FFFF responses, we begin to recognize how those responses feel in our bodies. Awareness of past behaviors can help shape our future reactions.

Ask yourself if there are reactions or behaviors you exhibit more frequently than the other FFFF responses. Are you someone who immediately fights back when stressed? Or are you heading out the door at the slightest indication of any friction? Do you find you always try to appease others to keep the peace? Or are you at a loss for words in heated discussions? Recognizing the warning signs and how your body feels under stress can help you calm yourself when you find yourself in situations that have the potential to activate your FFFF responses.

How does you body feel right at the moment of the inciting incident, when you know conflict is inevitable. You recognize there is friction and the flame of conflict it getting ready to ignite. Prior to fight or flight response kicks in, a person may feel extremely alert, agitated, aggressive, or like they need to leave a room or location. They have an overwhelming need to move or act. Before the freeze or fawn response, a person might notice their thinking and body slowing down or find they are grasping for ways to appease someone. They are looking for the exits in the room and grasping for ways to de-escalate the situation. Awareness of your patterns and how your body feels may help to thwart habitual reactions.

Brene Brown writes in her book, *Atlas of the Heart*, that in her "Dare to Lead" training, she asks participants what it looks like when they feel threatened in the workplace. The threat could be difficult feedback or an overwhelming workload they perceive is assigned to them unfairly.

Most people struggle to remember the exact thoughts and feelings, which makes sense, given that many of us go into a fight-or-flight mode in these situations.

> However, for the most part, people can remember their physical responses: Folding their arms over their chest, shoving their hands into their pockets, getting tunnel vision, feeling their heart race, looking down, and getting dry mouth are just a few. It's worth thinking about physical cues that show up for you when experiencing defensive and devising a strategy to help pull you back into the present moment.[49]

Brown goes on to share her strategy to disarm her defensiveness. She opens her palms and lets her arms fall to her side or onto her lap. Her open body positioning signals her brain that she is not in physical danger.

Awareness of how we typically respond helps develop a plan for what we can do if we find ourselves in true-life inciting incidents. Recognizing what our bodies feel like when our nervous system activates allows for early interventions and the ability to signal our bodies to calm down. There are even more preventative measures to be taken.

I have an example of learning from a past FFFF experience. I've learned my typical response to threat is to flee or fight. I know this about myself and have some exercises I do when I find myself in these situations. I share these exercises at the end of the chapter. The FFFF response that I personally experienced the least is the freeze response. For me, this is not my typical response, so I was not prepared for it when it happened, but I am now. With the fight, flight, and fawn response my reaction time is typically very fast, so fast in fact, that it is difficult for me to slow my responses. My experience with the freeze response was completely different. Everything moved in slow motion. Instead of my typical response of time speeding up, everything switched to sssslll-looooowwww motion. The feeling was bazaar and unfamiliar.

---

[49] Brown, *Atlas of the Heart*, 196

I was having a conversation with a good friend over a leisurely lunch. We had spent the day shopping together and stopped at the mall food court for a late lunch. I was relaxed and enjoying the day. She casually asked me if I planned to attend an event hosted by mutual friends. I replied, "Probably not." I started to share the reasons I didn't think I would go when I noticed her posture and demeanor change. Through squinting eyes and clenched jaws, she asked me how I could turn my back on my friends by not showing up for them. I'm sorry, what? She was angry and spoke aggressively about how this was a recurring pattern of behavior, not showing up for people, that I needed to check. I felt the world go into slow motion. I had tunnel vision, so all I saw were her squinty eyes. My brain stopped working. I mean, it flatlined. It wasn't just that I couldn't put two words together to form a sentence to save my soul, but it was like she was speaking a foreign language. I couldn't make sense of what she was saying. I now know that I was experiencing the freeze response. It was a long time before my brain came back online. I can only imagine what she saw from her side of the table. I felt like I was in a daze for the rest of our time together. Hours later, after being home and safe, I thought of everything I wished I'd said.

I know words were not available to me when I was in the moment, BUT this is a big but, I could have done some things in real time to help my brain and body calm down. I wish I had told myself to breathe and internally repeat the phrase, "There is no bear. There is no bear." In retrospect, I could have excused myself to the restroom to give myself time to snap out of it. This is a great tip when you need to buy yourself some time. People will not follow you into a bathroom stall. If they do, you have much bigger problems to deal with. Knowing what it feels like when my body experiences the freeze response will help me plan for the next time this happens.

We can plan for our responses, if we examine how we feel physically in acute stress. Our bodies alert us to potential danger. We have physical cues when our lids are flipping. It is like an internal alarm system screaming at us, "DANGER!" When facing stress or danger, our breathing becomes shallow. Our vision narrows. Muscles tighten. Jaws clench. We become hyper-aware of the situation, and time may slow down, or our responses may speed up.

In Chapter 1, there is a diagram of the climatic play structure. Prior to the rising tension, there is the moment when conflict was introduced. This moment is called the inciting incident. I marked this moment with a flame because this is the spark that sets the conflict in motion. "Between stimulus and response there is a space. In that space is our power to choose our response. In our response lies our growth and freedom."[50]

What can we do when we feel these physical cues indicating danger? We know conflict is about to start. Is there something we can do to help our flipped-lids?

Thoroughly understanding your body's natural fight or freeze or fawn response is a way to help cope with these situations. When you notice that your body becomes tense, there are steps you can take to try to calm and relax your body. There is no doubt that the fight or flight response has a distinct purpose and function, but non-threatening situations like work, bills, kids, finances, and health can be some of the largest, non-threatening stressors. Stress management is critical to your overall health. The stress response, and precisely the fight or flight or freeze or fawn response, is one of the major topics studied in health psychology. Experts in the field are interested in helping people discover ways to combat stress, which sometimes can be unnecessary, to live healthier, more fruitful lives. By understanding the fight or flight or freeze or fawn trigger more, psychologists are helping people uncover new strategies for dealing with the natural reaction of stress.[51]

Once we have flipped our lids, it can take 20 or more minutes to resume clear thinking. I remember an advertisement for bath salts

---

[50] Owens, *Love and Rage*, XIV

[51] Mia Belle Frothingham, "Fight, Flight, Freeze, or Fawn: What This Response Means," *Simply Psychology*, (October 6, 2021)

called Calgon. Calgon would turn the bath water a beautiful blue. The commercial had an exhausted woman sinking into an inviting tub of steaming blue water. The tagline was "Calgon, take me away." As it turns out, the advertisers were on to something. The only way to close your lid is to allow your nervous system time to regulate. You can do quite a few things in the moment or moments following a lid-flipping episode.

Here are some suggestions to try when you know you are experiencing the FFFF responses. The list comes from various sources gathered over many years. These are practical exercises that I can recommend from experience. I've done them, including going into a closet and shaking to taking my shoes off in public parks to ground myself. These are things to help get your nervous system to calm down.

- Breathe. When our brains and bodies perceive danger, breathing becomes shallow and fast. Changing our breath tells our brain we are okay. The Box Breathing technique is an exercise to help slow and focus our breath: breathe in for 4 beats, hold for 2, and breathe out for 4. Another exercise is to smell the soup and cool the soup. Breathe in like you are smelling soup, and then out your mouth like you're cooling the soup.
- Movement. Your muscles tighten and are on alert in case you need to flee a bear attack or worse. Any movement can help your body get rid of some of this energy. Tightening and releasing your fists under a table over and over or shaking your leg under a desk can be done discreetly. Jumping up and down or shaking your body also helps. Just move your body.
- Stand on solid ground, preferably barefoot, or stand or sit with your back against a wall. I know this sounds crazy, but it works. Your body feels secure with a solid surface beneath it, and your back is protected. Your body then cues you brain that you are safe.

- Mantras – Repeating to yourself a phrase that makes you feel safe. You could probably guess mine by now: There is no bear. There is no bear. And, breathe, just breathe, just breathe.
- Drink water. I know it sounds crazy, but it works. Drink a glass of water, preferably ice water.
- 5, 4, 3, 2, 1 meditation. In your mind, name 5 things you can see. 4 things you can hear. 3 things you can touch. 2 things you can smell. 1 thing you can taste. Repeat.

Recalling my encounter in the Cava restaurant when someone basically ordered me not to sit down and save a table? I knew I was under attack. My body was immediately on high alert. I did a couple of things to help my body know it was not in danger. Under the table, I started flexing my hands rapidly to release adrenaline. I broke eye contact with the woman and looked around. This helped me see that I was not alone and not in danger. Looking around also gave me time to process my surroundings, signaling to my body that I was in a safe space. I did not respond immediately and made myself pause; believe me, my body didn't feel like pausing; it wanted to react. I also looked down at the two value words I imagined tattooed on my arm: integrity and kindness. The FFFF responses were alive and well, but I did things to help start to close my lid. I took a few breaths and relaxed my facial muscles, saying, "We are just having a conversation and trying to decide what to do." I smiled at the woman and turned my full attention toward my friend and away from the woman.

My friend and I decided the restaurant was too loud and crowded for us to have a good visit with each other and left. As I got up and walked out the door, I felt controlled and composed. Once I got outside, however, I felt all the adrenaline and emotions: anger, embarrassment, disbelief, confusion. What in the world had just happened? Did I handle the situation perfectly? Could I have done something differently or better? I'm sure, but I responded well and learned some important things.

1. I knew my values and stayed consistent with them.
2. I used the tactics I had learned to help me when I felt the FFFF responses kick in. And they worked!
3. I also learned I needed to hear what the lady was actually saying. All I heard was the reprimand, but she did have a good point. It probably would work best if people didn't save tables. I've made a mental note that the next time I am confronted similarly, I will listen to the confronter. Get curious. Ask clarifying questions. I don't know that it would have changed the outcome, but it is a good tactic to help move from confrontation to conversation.

We will find ourselves in many battles we do not choose, but what about those things we deem worth the fight? How do we choose our battles? How do we decide what causes are worth taking the risk of purposefully entering conflict head-on? There are so many things worthy of confronting. It can be overwhelming. In the next chapter, we will explore how we know what battles we choose to enter or the ones we may even instigate.

Reflection and Discussion Questions:

- Kristy advocates that remembering our FFFF moments is valuable, as we can learn from them. Can you recall a time you flipped your lid? What "F" would you assign to the experience? How did your body feel as it was happening?
- Research shows that our brains can form new neuro-pathways and are malleable. Does this encourage you? What patterns would you change within yourself when it comes to conflict?
- Considering our ability to change how to respond and understand conflict, what's your strategy moving forward to be more compassionate towards yourself and others? How will you make

changes to improve the way you handle conflicts and other difficult situations?
- What are your warning signs that your brain is about to switch to FFFF response? What responses in your body can you identify?
- Kristy notes that it can take up to 20 minutes for our brains and bodies to return to a calm state once triggered. What coping skills do you lean on when you are in this state?
- Kristy outlines several research-backed coping strategies. What is a new one you can try out, and how might it help you?

Chapter 10

What is Worthy of the Fight?

> Choose your battles wisely. After all, life isn't measured by how many times you stood up to fight. It's not winning battles that makes you happy, but it's how many times you turned away and chose to look into a better direction. Life is too short to spend it on warring. Fight only the most, most, most important ones, let the rest go. –C. JoyBell C.

I HAVE STOPPED and started writing this chapter so many times. This is the chapter I have agonized over more than any other as I've asked myself and others: How do you choose your battles? I am not talking about minor conflicts; we face those conflicts regularly. A minor conflict might be a family member who talks too much or a person who never replaces toilet paper. These annoyances may seem significant when they happen, but a solution or some form of coping can be found relatively easily. I am referring to massive conflicts—those conflicts where solutions seem impossible. The hope of reconciliation and moving forward seems a distant dream. If a resolution to this conflict could actually be agreed upon, it would be life-changing or life-altering. The kind of conflict I'm referring to isn't a one-time encounter with a rude lady in a restaurant or a co-worker who is always late. These are the big wars you choose to enter on principle and conviction. The fight is not for personal gain but for the greater good.

"Pick Your Battles" is a familiar saying. The origin is unknown, but it implies battles are chosen and, at some point, battles must be fought. I agree with both these statements but hesitate to add fuel to what seems to be a time when explosive arguments and unproductive disagreements are the norm, expected, and seemingly required. I don't want to challenge people to take up a cause as much as to encourage all of us to turn down the volume and rhetoric of our discourses. Fight, yes! Scream, not so much. We need to have strong convictions, but like teachers who raise their voices too often, students cease to hear the teacher because they have grown accustomed to the noise. We have become desensitized to screaming because it happens all day, every day, 24/7.

We also seem stuck in a cycle of arguments. These arguments, for some reason, intrigue us and somehow suck us in and swallow us whole. Or at least swallow our brains and the ability to think rationally. In Amanda Ripley's glossary at the beginning of her book *High Conflict*, she defines "high conflict" as "a conflict that becomes self-perpetuating and all-consuming, in which almost everyone ends up worse off. Typically an us-versus-them-conflict."[52] I don't want to promote "high conflict." The goal is to learn how to enter, promote, and execute "good conflict."

That's the main difference between high conflict and good conflict.

> It's not usually a function of the subject of the conflict. Nor is it about the yelling. It's about stagnation. In healthy conflict, there is movement. Questions get asked. Curiosity exists. There can be yelling too. But healthy conflict leads somewhere. It feels more interesting to get to the other side than to stay in it. In high conflict, the conflict Is the destination. There's nowhere to go.[53]

---

[52] Ripley, *High Conflict*, Glossary

[53] Ripley, *High Conflict*, 27

What is Worthy of the Fight?

The structure of this chapter may seem contradictory. It will start with lots of caution and warning and a lot of wait, wait, wait, wait. It will finish with a charge to pick up your cross and fight the good fight. Forgive me for the mixed message; choosing and picking the battle are the most critical elements and criteria for fighting a good fight. Will life force us to fight at some point? Absolutely! Should we be discerning about when and why? You bet!

As such, how do we begin to pick our battles? What do we deem worthy of a fight? What warrants our involvement? How do we know what battles to walk away from or even run from? Which ones should we dive into full force and lead the charge? After stopping and starting this chapter, I finally thought I had what I presumed to be a fantastic epiphany. What would Jesus do? That's a good place to start, right? We've discussed His righteous anger and confrontations, but He wasn't always angry and fighting. He could have been, you know. There was plenty to stir Him to do lots of table flipping, but He only did that once. Why? How did He know what fights to enter or even provoke?

> Those who were accustomed to receiving VIP treatment, who sat at the head table at banquets, and who were esteemed in the temple and marketplace seemed not to be Jesus' primary focus. Instead, he turned his attention to those accustomed to being ignored, mistreated, discarded, and despised by the general public. If you were sick, poor, sexually damaged, or paralyzed by guilt and shame, for example, Jesus would move toward you and tell you what nobody else would: *you matter*.[54]

I hope all Christians would give a hearty amen to the above description of Jesus's priorities. He actively fought for the "ignored, mistreated, discarded, and despised," in a word, the marginalized. But here is the

---

[54] Sauls, *A Gentle Answer*, 4-5

rub: when Christians begin to discuss the marginalized, we have different ways of discerning and deciding who is mistreated, ignored, or discarded. The people often "despised by the general public" are not welcomed in churches. Christians are conflicted on how to deal with the "poor" and "sexually damaged." I hesitate even to write "sexually damaged" because the meaning attached to this phrase will be vastly different from person to person and potentially triggering to many who have experienced various kinds of sexual assault or trauma. Even conversing about loving our neighbors can turn ugly as we disagree on who our neighbors are. What seems simple in reality becomes so complicated. I want to care for others the way Jesus would, but you and I may differ on what this looks like.

I hope this chapter ends with such an inspiring charge for all to find and enter their specific battles with such gusto that the reader will rush to dress in the shiny armor of God, holding the shield of faith and wielding the sword of the Spirit. I feel like a sleek white horse would be a nice addition, but that is not Biblical, so I will push down the impulse of an equestrian suggestion. The passage that holds the description of "The Armor of God" has believers preparing for war. Reading the verse, one could get swept away with fighting for righteousness' sake. But Ephesians 6:12 puts a qualifier on who we are fighting. "For our struggle is not against flesh and blood, but against the rulers, against the authorities, against the powers of this dark world, and against the spiritual forces of evil in the heavenly realms" (Ephesians 6:10-18 NIV). Even though it can be hard to remember and does not often feel true, our battle is not against each other, but at times, that is exactly what it ends up being.

Many years ago, dear friends answered the call to leave their home and family to be missionaries in Spain. They desired to share Christ with the world, literally. This husband and wife inspired me, but even as they raised funds for the upcoming venture to go to the other side of the world, the wife's belly was swelling with their first child. They were leaving the beautiful state of Colorado and taking their firstborn far away from their family. I cannot imagine how difficult this decision must have been. This couple has now been full-time missionaries for over 30 years. Today, they are team leaders overseeing more than 200 missionaries, which I'm sure is beyond a full-time job. I was recently talking with these friends via Zoom. They shared with me that the number one reason people leave the mission field is because missionaries often find they can't get along with their team members. Let this sink in a minute. I'll join you in the next paragraph.

Men and women who have left their homes, families, and culture and dedicated themselves to full-time ministry leave their calling because they don't get along with others. I felt like the air had been knocked out of me when I heard this. Whoooosh! Of all people, I would think that missionaries would be unified by their shared faith and calling. How quickly we can all lose sight of the edifying and unifying life of Jesus Christ. If you have ever worked or lived with another person, you know it's not always simple or easy to maintain common ground.

It's Not Always Simple

It is the end of October, as I am writing, which means all things fall and Halloween. Thankfully, the weather has finally turned cool in central Texas. This past Sunday, I taught the Pumpkin Gospel, a children's book, to kids in grades kindergarten through 5th. My assignment was to teach an object lesson involving a pumpkin that introduced the children to the Roman Road to salvation in ten minutes. The systematic steps to eternal life with Jesus were boiled down to three easy steps: ABC: A – Admit to God you are a sinner. B – Believe that perfect Jesus died on the cross to forgive your sins. C – Choose to follow Jesus. Simple, right? Ha!

My lesson began by saying, "We are just like pumpkins!" *(What? We are nothing like pumpkins, but I've already started down this road. Too late to back out now. I am confident that I can spin this so the kids will think they are similar to a pumpkin.)* I continued, "We are all different shapes and sizes, and just like you might have chosen the pumpkins you have at home, God chooses each of us." *(Ok. Pretty good start.)* "We may clean the outsides of a pumpkin straight from the field, but the real mess is on the inside. Just like all of us, pumpkins have yucky stuff on the inside." *(Ok, wait. That doesn't sound good.)* "It's not like we are all bad, but we sometimes do bad things. Even if we don't intend to be bad, it just sometimes happens. Right? Do you ever do bad things? Inside of us, we have sin. Just like a pumpkin has a mess inside, we also have messy insides, sin. Sin is anything not pleasing to God, and it can be messy like the inside of a pumpkin." *(I am now rambling.)* "Can a pumpkin clean its insides? No? Well, we can't clean our sins by ourselves, either. We need help." *(At this point, I am scooping the gross pumpkin innards out of the pumpkin and putting it on a paper plate. I get a whiff of the inside of the pumpkin and try not to gag. My face says it all. It feels and smells awful. The kids are thrilled at my response and the grossness of the pumpkin.)* "Of course, our insides don't look anything like this. *(This is where it really starts falling apart. I look into these trusting baby faces and realize they are concrete thinkers. Do they think our insides look like pumpkin guts?)* "Jesus cleans out our insides, and we are transformed more and more into His likeness." *(Do you think they are picturing a large hand coming down from heaven and scooping out their insides? At this point, I pretend to cut a Jack-O-Lantern-type face already pre-cut on the side of the pumpkin they can't see. I turn the face so the kids can see a stereotypical grinning Jack-O-Lantern.)* "So that to the rest of the world, we look more like Jesus. Of course, Jesus doesn't really look like a pumpkin. Of course, we don't really look like this either." *(Oh, good grief! This sounded so good at home.)* "And then Jesus lives inside of us, and we shine our light for all to see." *(At this point, I put a flashlight into the pumpkin.)* "Ok. Listen. We don't really glow like a pumpkin….." *(I wanted to end with, "Ok, look, we really aren't anything like pumpkins!!")* Sigh. I really did start with the best intentions. I think it ended up being an okay object lesson, and hopefully, the small group leaders cleared up any confusion, but I would love to hear how kids re-told what they had learned that morning on their way home from church. What I thought was a simple concept was much more complicated. When we simplify things and distill them into sound bites or simple solutions, we will probably get some things wrong, even when we have the best intentions.

Few things in life are simple. Most things are layered and complex. I wish I could see all issues in simple, straightforward terms, so simple that a first-grader could understand. I want to get to the heart of issues so that I can pick the correct side, the right side. Adopting the same dress code used in old Western movies could be helpful. If you are the bad guy, you wear a black hat, the good guy, a white one. Conflicts are often more nuanced and rarely black or white, right or wrong, good or evil.

In recent years, I have sat across dinner tables looking at the familiar faces of family and friends in shock at how we view various topics differently. I had no idea how much we differed! How can two parties with similar backgrounds and respect for each other have such widely disparate opinions? We have the same information, and yet we land on different sides. So, which side is right and which is wrong? We can have the best intentions in discerning complex issues with the knowledge and resources available and come up with vastly different solutions. Sometimes, we don't even agree on what the problem is.

We live on a broken planet. There are so many needs, too many. There is so much worth fighting for or against. Here is a small sampling of the complex issues we face today: the inclusion/exclusion of the LBGQT+ community, immigration/secure borders, gun control/the right to bear arms, separation of church and state/prayer in schools, the rights of the unborn/the rights a woman, freedom of speech/government censorship, welfare state/free market and on and on. The list is endless and can feel overwhelming. As you read the list, some causes may resonate with you more than others. You may know where you stand on one issue and cannot condone the opposing side's stance. Deep down in your heart, you wonder about people with an opposing view, "How can they have gotten it so WRONG? Where did their life go so far off track!"

Some causes you might not deem worthy of your time, but others are the hill you would choose to die upon. I think we can agree that many things are worth "falling on your sword," but we don't always agree on the causes or issues. It is also good to acknowledge that falling on a sword can kill you; even if it doesn't, it will hurt…a lot! Unlike cats, we don't have nine lives. I have always thought everyone should be allotted two rants on any social platform a year. That's all—just two. I think we might only get to fall on our sword once or twice in a lifetime.

The whole concept of "falling on your sword" is a one-way trip. You get one chance to make a point of that magnitude. Historically, "falling on your sword" meant physically driving a sword through your mid-section with no hope for survival. This extreme purpose was to prevent capture, make the ultimate sacrifice, or make a dramatic statement. Guess what–You only get to do this once.

I've known people who relish making loud and aggressive statements over and over. It is exhausting. They are exhausting. Ultimately, their opinions become empty because no one is listening to them. We can get caught up in the desire to fix all the problems in the world. News Flash! It is not your job to save the world. Leave the world-saving to God, and choose your sword-falling and hill-dying wisely.

I do not want to diminish the profound needs of others or the importance of our calling to be the world's light. We need to be Jesus' hands and feet. We are Jesus with "skin on" to the world. I certainly don't want to go through life driving in neutral, not moving forward, just spinning my wheels, but I also want to be cautious about rushing into conflict when emotions are high and rational thought is long gone.

> *"This generation is the first to* turn hate into an asset." When Dr. John Perkins, the eighty-nine-year-old Christian minister and civil rights icon/activist, said these words at a recent leaders' gathering in Nashville, things I've

been feeling about the current state of Western society came into sharper focus. For many years now, I've grown increasingly perplexed over what feels like a culture of suspicion, mistrust, and us-against-them. Whatever the subject may be – politics, sexuality, immigration, income gaps, women's concerns, race, or other social matters over which people have differences – angst, suspicion, outrage, and outright hate increasingly shape our response to the world around us.[55]

I am reminded of a phrase I heard a seasoned Bible teacher say to warn a younger Christian teacher about condemning others too quickly in their stance on a specific issue. Her advice was to remember that what the younger was teaching was fragile. It was new fruit. Meaning it might not be ready for some to accept and consume. More time was needed for this new approach to ministry to be widely accepted. Sometimes, the best advice is to start small and slow. As much as I want to heed the call to advocate for needed change, I also want to hit pause and warn: many battles are not yours to fight, and, honestly, many battles may not be worth the fight. There are times when fighting the wrong cause at the wrong time can make things worse.

<u>Don't be a Bully</u>

I heard someone share a story about their father whose health was failing. He was recounting his dad's retirement party. The retirement party was held at a nice restaurant, and colleagues, friends, and family had gathered to celebrate his dad. The son admittedly referred to himself as a bit of a hothead in his early years. His memory of the entire event is sitting at a table with his dad, embroiled in a rather heated, lengthy debate. With much sadness and regret, the son realized he

---

[55] Sauls, *Gentle Answer*, XVII

had monopolized his father for the whole evening on a night meant to honor his dad, and what was most tragic was that years later, he couldn't even remember what the two were arguing about. Isn't that sad? I don't know about you, but I can relate. I don't want my words and actions to be fruitless. Life is too precious to waste on futile and insignificant arguments.

Fighting for everything all of the time is exhausting and unproductive. It's not productive because people don't want to be around someone always fighting and angry. No one likes an argumentative person. An argumentative person is someone who loves to pick a fight. They know where to poke someone to start an all-out brawl for no reason other than to fight. They like it. They want to be the aggressor, the bully. No one else enjoys these exchanges. Trust me. I've asked. We all know these people. We've sat across from them at too many holiday dinners. They are the people you try not to make eye contact with at the grocery store, hoping they don't see you. You fervently pray you never have to serve on a committee with them or get invited to the same gatherings.

I've known my fair share of people that I would put in the argumentative category. I have covertly asked argumentative people if they like people who constantly argue, always wanting to prove they are right and everyone else is wrong. Guess what? They all immediately said, "No!" They then brought up someone they thought was argumentative and criticized them for their abrasive and often repulsive behavior. Interesting. The people I would describe as argumentative don't like people who fight just for the sake of fighting. If you like heated, loud, and unresolved conflict, you might be the person others are avoiding. It's worth considering.

An argumentative person's end game is to dominate the conversation, prove they are right, and win at all costs. Their aggressive manner does not produce good fruit. Their discussions are unproductive because the aggressor repels others and shuts communication down. These are the people you know are best to refrain from engaging. It's not worth it. You know how the conversation is going to go before it even starts. If you desire positive change and productive exchanges, screaming and finger-pointing are not constructive, nor is engaging with these people.

Know Your Triggers

What behavior of others sets your teeth on edge? You know what I'm talking about. That thing that makes your mad meter go from 0 to 100 in no time at all. Is it the person that thinks they know everything, the know-it-all? Do you find yourself bristling if you catch even a whiff of condescension in the air? Is it a lack of trust, faith, or acceptance from others? Maybe for you, it's the co-worker who dumps on you or takes credit for your work.

Triggers can multiply if we are tired, hungry, or busy. Triggers can also be ignited by situations that conjure up memories we desperately wish would go away. When we are triggered, just like a gun that is cocked, we are ready to go off. Our defenses go up. We are primed to shoot off our mouths aimed at the guilty party or innocent bystander.

What is that thing that pushes your buttons? Or who is that person that knows how to push your buttons? We all have buttons. We really do. For the sake of transparency, I will tell you mine: I cannot stand it when someone tells me what to do. Man, oh, man, just writing that makes my blood temperature go up a few degrees. Now, if you have the authority to ask me to do something, I am fine with that. A boss, a teacher, and even some elders have my blessing and permission to instruct me, but if you are just Joe Schmo standing on the street, I do not like to be told what to do. It is a trigger for me, and I know it. And knowing is half the battle.

Once you know what annoys you, makes you defensive, or just flat-out mad, you can recognize it in real-time. Step back. Breathe. Reassess before you go off half-cocked. Knowing may be more than half the battle. Preparation is key.

There is No Bear. Just Breathe.

<u>Herd Mentality</u>

We are herd animals. It's true. Humans are herd animals. We live in packs and rely on each other for safety and survival. Herd behavior can be seen especially on display in times of panic or danger… or Texas high school football games. If you have ever participated in live entertainment, you've experienced herd behavior when at the end of a moving performance, an audience will rise to their feet in unison for a standing ovation, or perhaps there is a moment of quiet stillness before the applause begins. The audience demonstrates the seemingly orchestrated effect of a unified response to a shared experience. Crowds often have the same response in victory, appreciation, silent anticipation, and bad calls made by refs.

As a nation, we witnessed extreme herd mentality on January 6, 2021, as a mob attacked the U.S. Capitol. They descended on the building like a hive of angry hornets, engulfing buildings and pouring into broken windows. Be warned: emotions and reactions can be extremely contagious. Be careful of being swept up in a crowd response. If left to your own devices, without the input of others, would you respond the same way if you were alone? Is this your cause or the cause of others? Will you regret your decision or actions later?

It is easy to be swept away in a crowd. Anxiety, fear, and anger can spread through people like wildfire, consuming all in its path. After a fire, there is nothing left but ash and debris. New growth happens over time, but restoring a forest to its former glory after a fire will take years. Be careful of shared heightened passion and emotion. Step back. Breathe. Walk away if necessary. The Most Reverend Michael B. Curry wrote the following in his beautiful book, *Love Is The Way*.

If I reacted in anger, I would add more destructive anxiety to the situation. I knew enough about human nature to know that a sense of safety, not anxiety, is what puts people in a space to open their hearts to change.[56]

Personal Bias

Personal bias is tricky to unpack and uncover because it refers to unconscious beliefs or attitudes. These beliefs are so much a part of how we see and perceive the world that we are unaware of them. As much as we cringe to think we have any bias about people based on age, gender, or race, we most likely do. Previously, I shared that people may have preconceived notions that the poor are lazy while others believe the rich are selfish and greedy. What about a person's appearance? Do you react differently to someone who is exceptionally pleasing to the eye? The Business Insider reported in 2018 that there were benefits for men and women who were considered physically attractive. The report shares people scientifically perceived as attractive had a greater chance of landing better jobs. Attractive people were also considered more trustworthy, smarter, healthier, and happier. However, "when attractive female participants applied for a 'traditionally masculine' role, they were less likely to be hired than both men and unattractive women."[57]

How do we overcome our own bias? Like so many things, awareness is the first step, and then it takes intention, time, trial and error, and, most importantly, a willingness to grow and change. Certainly, before entering a huge battle, it is good to try and look at the issue from all sides. The old saying to "walk in another person's shoes" is a good one. Paul talks about becoming all things to all people so that they might know Christ. I don't think this was Paul shape-shifting or trying to be

---

[56] Bishop Michael Curry, *Love is the Way: Holding on to Hope in Troubling Times*, (New York, Avery an imprint of Penguin Random House, 2020) 182

[57] "What are the Examples of Personal Biases," *Impactly, A Vector Solutions Company*, https://www.getimpactly.com/post/examples-of-personal-biases#

deceitful. It was more about understanding and relating to the people God put in his path. Could he see the world from their point of view? How best could he relate to all people?

> To the Jews I became like a Jew, to win the Jews. To those under the law I became like one under the law (though I myself am not under the law), so as to win those under the law. To those not having the law I became like one not having the law (though I am not free from God's law but am under Christ's law), so as to win those not having the law. To the weak I became weak, to win the weak. I have become all things to all people so that by all possible means I might save some.
> 1 Corinthians 9:20-22 (NIV)

Understanding Our Beliefs

I was sitting in a diner early on a Saturday morning with two friends. I was drooling over the pancakes I wanted on the menu, knowing I would most likely order the lighter veggie omelet option. My diet mentality is hard for me to overcome. One of my friends was distracted and looking around the restaurant, "Look at all these men wearing baseball hats inside a building." I looked around, and sure enough, there were men of all ages with caps on their heads. They are old enough to know better! Everyone knows you don't wear hats inside, right? This observation began a discussion on some unseen rule book that the three of us sitting at the table had read – or we had read to us. Why can't men wear hats inside? Where did that rule come from? None of us knew the origin of this rule. We just knew it and followed it. That led to our discussion of wearing white after Labor Day. What was the reason for this declaration that I rigidly conformed to for many years without asking why I was doing it? And don't get me started on place settings, elbows on the table, wearing black to weddings, and many other "rules"

I was taught growing up. I never asked why. I just knew what was right or wrong because someone told me so.

I could fill these pages with lists and lists of things I thought were true only because I'd heard someone say it. Or because I sat under someone who was teaching it as gospel truth. The danger with taking what others say at face value is that we often live in echo chambers of people like us repeating things we want to be true. In our youth, we are instructed on what is right by others, and rightly so. We don't come out of the womb knowing everything. We have to be taught. This is as it should be, but at some point, we need to think for ourselves and make up our own minds. The traditions and beliefs that have become familiar, comfortable, and habitual need to be examined and questioned, or you could end up being some grumpy old lady sitting in a diner condemning men for wearing hats inside! Oh, I so don't want to be that woman!!

Now, I'm not saying that etiquette is wrong; far from it. And if I send you a gift, I expect a thank you note. But you see, there are reasons for my request. How will I know if you ever received the gift? And it is kind and thoughtful to thank someone. I know this to be true. Question your beliefs. This will not weaken your values or beliefs but grow your convictions as you pull them apart and understand them better. Are you like the Hatfields and McCoys, never asking why you actively despise the other family? You just know you do because……it's just always been that way. Too often, we fight for the causes of our families or cultures without personal convictions or understanding.

Make sure you do your homework before taking a side or entering a fight. Just because it's on the internet doesn't mean it's true. How many times have we witnessed something go viral only to discover it wasn't based in fact? I am guilty of re-posting things I originally read on a media outlet or from someone I knew and respected before doing my fact-finding, only to discover I was complicit in spreading false information. Once you share something via the World Wide Web, you can't ever really take it back. It will have been seen by someone, somewhere.

Information today can be distributed instantly to millions of people with one click. Make sure you know what you are sharing. Do your homework. Check the facts before you click.

What Does the Bible Say?

This will be my last and final caution. Before you throw your hat in the ring, know what the Bible says about the issue. Please, do not do what my younger self was so prone to do. I would dive headfirst into an argument. I was passionate, and most likely angry about something or felt slighted in some way, and wanted to win so badly that I would flip through my Bible's glossary trying to find a verse to support my argument and ensure my victory while looking saintly and holy at the same time. This is embarrassing but true. I approached conflict this way for years. This is called weaponizing scripture. Think about that. I was using the Word of God for selfish purposes and personal gain. Oh, Lord, forgive me. I knew exactly what I was doing. I wanted to be right and win more than I wanted to be humble and godly.

I'm unsure when it completely sunk in that a verse out of context could be dangerous and harmful, but it can. Scripture has been used to promote slavery and nation dominating nation. It has been used to subjugate wives to their husbands, children to parents, and lay people to church leaders. The Bible has been used to make people do things it never, ever intended. The Bible gives insight into the heart and mind of God. Use it carefully. Use it well.

I am in no way a Bible scholar. I do NOT have all the answers. I do NOT know everything. Friend, I advise staying away from those who think they do know it all. My warning is that before you fight for something, know what the Bible says about it and study it well. The best way to prevent misinterpretation is to read every passage that deals with an issue and then read the surrounding passages. Listen to "experts" on various subjects and not just the ones you agree with. Yikes! Yep. Listen to what the opposing side has to say. Don't listen to one podcast. Listen to multiple. Don't follow one teacher but many. Surround yourself with people who will speak good and hard truth to you and bring you up short when needed.

A Call to Act

Dr. John Gottman says, "A relationship without conflict is a relationship without communication and is bound to fail. Conflict is inevitable whenever two or more people are talking about things from their own perspectives. Disagreements are a sign that the relationship's soil is healthy."[58]

Avoidance is an option. You can sit on the sidelines, giving everyone and everything a pass for bad behavior and a Southern, "Bless their heart." I've heard this extreme neutrality called weaponizing grace, meaning that granting grace to everyone, even if they behave contrary to your values and belief system, is not holding people accountable for their actions. If there are no consequences for bad behavior, your neutrality permits the bad behavior. Silence makes you complicit. Ignoring problems can be a good tactic and is sometimes needed, but a passive approach to life will eventually cause problems.

Sweden has long been known for its neutrality, refusing to be involved directly in any armed conflicts. They remained passive until their neutrality threatened their peace. When Russia invaded Ukraine on February 24, 2022, Sweden looked outside their borders and saw that they were isolated and vulnerable. They realized they had no allies because of their professed neutrality. Russia was too close in proximity, like next door close. Sweden felt vulnerable, scared, and alone. Sweden started knocking on NATO's door, screaming, "Let us in! Let us in!"

We all can feel inadequate and unprepared for the work before us. Maybe we secretly pray someone else will step up so we won't have to. We wait for someone else to respond and plead, "Not me, Lord. Please, not me." But if not me, then who? If not us, then who? If not you, then who?

---

[58] Buster Benson, *Why are We Yelling?: The Art of Productive Disagreement*, (New York, Portfolio/Penguin, an Imprint of Peguin Random House, 2019) 8

The Reverend Allan Boesak of South Africa, who fought against apartheid, once said that when we go before God at the end of our lives to be judged, God will ask, "Where are your wounds?" Too many of us will say, "We have no wounds." Then God will ask, "Was nothing worth fighting for?"[59]

Can you imagine what would have happened if the leaders of the early church, the likes of Paul, Peter, James, and John, had looked at their past faults and failings and decided they were not the men to preach or spread the gospel? Honestly, they would have been justified to excuse themselves from ministry. We've talked about Peter being too quick to act at times and then not acting quickly enough at other times. Paul, a prominent figure in the early church and author of many books of the Bible, was at one time the person the early church thought would have been the last person to preach love and compassion, but God felt differently. James, Jesus' own brother, did not even acknowledge Jesus as Christ until after the resurrection. These three could have easily said, "No way! Not me! I am not worthy. I have made too many mistakes. I have gotten it wrong so many times before. Remember, God? Remember how I have messed up so many times?"

What is Yours to Do?

How do we begin to choose our actions with so many vital issues on the table? What areas need our involvement? What is your work to do? What is worth your time and effort? What causes should you walk away from? I can't tell you precisely what battle is yours to enter, but I can lead you through some questions that have helped me clarify and solidify my convictions and involvement.

---

[59] Brett, *Be the Miracle*, 65

Clarifying Questions for Choosing Your Battle:

1. What are you passionate about? What gets your juices flowing?
2. Will this matter to you in 5, 10, 20 years? Is it really that important? Is this something you can say has some eternal significance? Will it impact future generations?
3. What is your motivation for involvement? Is it to be right? Is it to gain notoriety? Or are your reasons selfless and godly?
4. What background and experiences have equipped you to work on various causes or with specific people groups?
5. How has God gifted you in certain areas? What skills do you uniquely possess that equip you for this work?
6. Have you done your homework and know about this issue from various resources? Have you listened to varying viewpoints?
7. If you currently don't have the education or training needed to meet a certain need, are you willing to study and train to gain the necessary knowledge and skills?
8. What words have you chosen to distill down your values? What values are figuratively tattooed on your arm? Do these causes line up with your values? Does this cause point back to the plumbline of your life?
9. Are you in a healthy enough place that you can think clearly? Do you have the time and space to give to this endeavor adequately? If not, what are you willing/able to clear off your plate? Are you in this for the long haul?
10. What are your triggers and personal biases?
11. What does the Bible say about this issue?
12. Have you prayed and asked God if this is your work to do?

Chapter 11

Church Conflict: Not Mine to Do

> Give us discernment in the face of troubling reports.
> Give us discernment to know when to pray,
> when to act, and when to simply shut off our screens and devices,
> and to sit quietly in your presence, casting the burdens of this world
> upon the strong shoulder of the one who alone is able to bear them up. Amen.[60]

FROM THE TIME I was two weeks old, I attended church twice on Sundays, once on Wednesdays, and on a good week, we returned for socials on the weekends. The rhythm of Sunday mornings was as soothing to me as swinging on my porch swing. The familiar gatherings with my chosen church family are still a time for me to re-focus and take in deep, fresh breaths, preparing me for the week ahead. I love the church. If it were ever to go away, I would miss it terribly. It would be naïve of me to think the church will stay the same for all eternity. I know God will always be who He is, but it is no secret that churches in America are changing. The American church is also declining.

Forty million Americans have stopped attending church in the past 25 years. That's something like 12 percent of the population, and

---

[60] McKelvey, *Every Moment Hole*, 162.

it represents the largest concentrated change in church attendance in American history.[61]

> As of 2021, the number of "religious nones"—people who don't identify with any established religion—in the U.S. had grown to nearly 30 percent of the population while professing Christians constituted 63 percent, down from 75 only a decade ago. The Pew Research Center recently projected the future of this trend: In three of its four scenarios, the percentage of Christians plunges to less than half the population by 2070, and in none does the trend reverse and the Church grow.[62]

I am not going to presume to have answers to the big questions of why churches are in decline or why there is so much division within churches and denominations. Much information can be found written by qualified people grappling with these issues. The conflicts facing churches are vast, and congregations are dividing rapidly. I can go down a rabbit hole of worry about the church's future, or I can choose to be proactive in my involvement and commitment to help the institution to the best of my ability, but what is my best? What is my work to do within the church that I dearly love?

Church Nostalgia: A Walk Down Memory Lane

My family attended Beacon Hill Baptist Church, and by family, I mean my immediate family as well as grandparents, aunts, uncles, and cousins—the whole lot. On the cover of the bulletin passed out each

---

[61] Jake Meader, "The Misunderstood Reason Millions of People Stopped Going to Church," *The Atlantic* (July 29, 2023), https://www.theatlantic.com/ideas/archive/2023/07/christian-church-communitiy-participation-drop/674843/

[62] Jake Meader, "The Misunderstood Reason Millions of People Stopped Going to Church."

Sunday was a picture of a hill with sun rays breaking through a cloudy sky. Each week, we would be handed a blue-tinted bulletin emitting the intoxicating smell of mimeograph machine ink. I loved that smell. The smell from the ink may have been the culprit for the spiritual high I got every Sunday morning. I loved going to church.

My mother sang in the choir, and my father was an usher, so I got to sit with various people, mainly my grandmother, during the sermon. Sometimes, I got to sit with the preacher's wife and children. I guess the preacher's wife was required to wear hose, heels, and pearls because that is what she wore every Sunday. I realize now that our little church surely did not pay them enough to keep her dressed in this finery. Maybe she had a couple of outfits she wore on a rotating schedule, but my memory of her is coifed perfection. In the winter months, she would wear black gloves with big rings worn on the outside of the gloves. I remember thinking it looked both elegant and strange.

When my mother had choir practice after prayer meetings on Wednesday nights, I often went home with my dad. He always made grilled cheese sandwiches with lots of butter and Campbell's Tomato Soup. I liked these Wednesday nights just fine, but the best Wednesdays were when I got to stay at the church and wait for my mom to finish choir practice. This is when I explored the church with my friend, Diana Gail. I guess the adults weren't too concerned about us running unsupervised through an empty building.

I felt like I owned Beacon Hill Baptist Church. I knew I wasn't the sole owner and gladly shared possession of the building with the rest of the congregation, but I knew its complex floor plan like the back of my hand. Church was a second home. It was as natural for me to roam the deserted halls of the church as it was my own backyard. Church was fun! Church was where friendships were made and adventures were had. Special events held in the basement, like fall festivals and potluck suppers, were the pinnacle of my social calendar. I wouldn't have wanted to be anywhere else.

I made a profession of faith and "walked the aisle" when I was nine. The Sunday of my baptism was particularly cold, and for some reason, the water heater decided not to work. I guess my baptism was already typed into the bulletin, so the schedule was not changing. It was written in permanent blue ink that I would be baptized that cold day in January. Why someone didn't declare that I shouldn't get into freezing cold water, I will never know, but I don't remember any discussion or choice given about getting dunked that day. The preacher met me in the middle of the baptistry, warm in his chest-high waders. I, however, was dressed in a t-shirt and shorts under an oversized white robe. I was so cold my teeth were chattering, and my fingers turned blue. It was not a spiritual moment for me. I was freezing. For some reason, we didn't take the time to blow dry my hair afterward, and I sat through the service with wet hair, still shivering. What I recall of that day is that I thought I'd never be physically warm again, but I remember the warming of my heart from all of the hugs and loud proclamations of "welcome to the family." I was celebrated and loved. And I didn't want to be anywhere else in the world.

The first time I took communion, my mom sat with me instead of singing in the choir. She carefully ensured I had my little cracker wafer and juice cup and passed the silver serving trays without incident. Unfortunately, I choked on the grape juice, but my mother was there assuring me, patting my back, and telling me that all was fine.

My church memberships have changed through the years as I've moved to different towns at varying stages of my life, but I have always attended and served in a church. As the years passed, I was the one singing in youth choirs and helping with vacation bible school. The church of my adolescent years was a bit of a departure from the bulletin-led childhood church. I thought we had entered a new level of holiness, when we visited Manor Baptist Church when I was probably twelve. The sanctuary lights were dim, and the preacher would end each service by raising his hands and speaking a blessing over us. I raised my face up to heaven and swear I felt God's favor rain down on me as

I heard, "May the Lord bless you and protect you. The Lord make his face shine on you and be gracious to you. The Lord lift up his face to you and grant you peace." (Numbers 6:24-26)

In my youth, I spent even more time in church than I did as a child. I was still there twice on Sunday and every Wednesday. This new fancy church had Wednesday night dinners before prayer meetings and youth activities. Youth retreats and summer camps took precedence over any school activities or work schedules. I wouldn't have had it any other way. I actually felt sorry for others who did not have a church home. What did one do with so much time on their hands? I could not imagine.

I cherish my Christian heritage. I know I have been blessed to grow up in a home rooted in the security of knowing God is on His throne and in control. There is a danger, however, in a nostalgic view of Christianity. We can get stuck in the past and be unwilling to change and do things differently. We can limit our vision to traditions and habits and be too comfortable in our rose-colored glasses. It is easy to forget church business is not always rosy or easy.

The church is the people. People are messy. The church will have its messy times as we navigate the complexities of life together. Church conflict: It's not fun but, it's inevitable.

I had an experience over twenty years ago that shaped my view on involvement in church politics and conflict. As so often happens, this learning and growing experience was painful, messy, and quite honestly embarrassing. I want to say I'm thankful for the lessons, but the memories are painful to revisit. However, I do think the lessons learned are worth sharing. One of the critical lessons learned is not every need must be met by me.

Fighting Someone Else's Battle

Years ago, one of the biggest challenges facing some churches was worship styles. I knew many, many wonderful people who were very passionate about this topic. Many musicians and choir members couldn't imagine a Sunday morning without choir robes and pipe organs. Others wanted to try to capture the emotional high of summer camps with familiar choruses and a more relaxed style. The hope was that this latter style would appeal to younger people. This debate was fundamentally important to many. For some, music was their conduit to a holy and intimate time with God. The time set aside for singing and special music was their "worship." Sunday morning worship was when they felt they could commune best with their heavenly Father. Old hymns comforted many in times of extreme grief or pain. The words of familiar songs were etched into their marrow, grounding them in traditions of the past. For others, choruses and phrase repetition were favored because of its simplicity. Some felt the lack of complex music and wording helped lead them into a time of worship.

Intellectually, I knew and understood the debate on worship styles. I understood that for some, this was a big, big deal. As a matter of fact, to many, it was a deal-breaker or dealmaker when choosing church membership. The stakes were just not that high for me.

If you were to tell me I had to choose between music or sermons each Sunday, for some reason there couldn't be both, I would choose the sermon. The spoken word is more powerful to me. In the car, I listen to podcasts much more than music. When I walk or clean the house, I have someone talking in my ear, not singing. However, my position on worship styles came into question in the early 2000's.

At the church we attended in May 2002, our long-time beloved minister of music retired, and the church faced the daunting task of replacing him. A Minister of Music Search Committee was formed. I was nominated to be on the committee. I declined the nomination because my schedule was too full, and I lacked knowledge and experience in church music and choir programs. I knew I was nominated because I had done some drama/skits on Sunday mornings and helped with Christmas musicals and Easter pageants, but I really didn't feel qualified to pick a minister of music. *(Lesson One: Decide what is your work to do and then say yes or no. Pray, gather information, talk to trusted sources, and then make a decision. Don't be swayed by the arguments of others. We all have work to do. Neither you nor I can do everything and do it well).*

Someone from the Nomination Committee called me at home and asked if I would be willing to serve. I said I would think about it, but deciding didn't take long. I called and declined the nomination ... and not long after, my phone started ringing and ringing. Many people wanted me, and I mean really, really wanted me on that committee. I was told I would be an invaluable member as I could be the one to make sure we got the person we needed to bring our church together. I am not overstating when I say this was a hot topic in our church. Our congregation was divided over the issue of worship style. I was told the other nominated committee members were too heavily weighted on the traditional side. I needed to fight for progression and change. I was told the contemporary worship style is what the younger generation needed, or our church would surely die. The life of our church was on the line! Others emphasized that we needed a minister who could do both worship styles. How else could the church ever hope to worship together? I was told I was the only one who could bridge the gap. I remember feeling like Esther. I was made "for such a time as this." I felt the important call to save my people. Let me interject here that the call wasn't from God but from people.

Well, what can I say? Their tactics, dare I say manipulation, worked. Oh, my ego loved the strokes it was getting. It was all up to me because I was so important. If not me, then who? I was the person to carry the church during this critical juncture. My inflated ego was soon deflated. It wasn't long before I knew I had made a colossal mistake. *(Lesson Two: Pride really does come before a fall).*

To this day, my time on that committee is one of my biggest regrets. It was not my work to do. It's not that I didn't care about music styles. There were just others who cared so much more. I wasn't the person for the time-consuming and often contentious job of weekly meetings, travel, and lengthy debates. I was clumsy in my arguments because the convictions I professed to be critically important were not my own. I was fighting for a cause that I didn't fully understand or own. And I mean, I fought.

I literally felt like a prizefighter in the corner of a ring, with different people speaking in my ear and telling me to go into every meeting ready for a fight. I was told stories about the other "side." "They" would win the battle at any cost. I heard rumors about different committee members' bad tempers and underhanded ways. They would fight dirty, so I had better be prepared to do the same. I needed to go in and be aggressive and win! So much depended on it. I was primed and ready for a fight! And fight I did, poorly, aggressively, and not graciously at all. *(Lesson Three: Don't listen to gossip and rumors. Make up your own mind about people and situations. I don't remember any underhandedness or bad dispositions from other members, and many became good friends).*

Baptist churches are committee-led. This means lay people have a huge say in every decision made concerning the church. I entered the Minister of Music Search Committee with an agenda. I knew I was right, and I was going to prove it. I did not listen open-mindedly to others on the committee. I was argumentative. Yep, I was that person. My pre-conceived rightness missed the magic of people working together for the greater good. I missed the opportunity to focus on what was best for our church. I also missed the opportunity to learn and be curious about the thoughts and opinions of others. I also did not lean into the musicians' expertise on the committee. I could have gained so much knowledge and insight from them. As painful as it is for me to now admit, I was arrogant, emotionally immature, and an obstacle to the committee's success. God can take our feeble attempts and make things work together for good. He is certainly more than able to do this, but this time, He let us fail, which, in retrospect, was for our good. Life's lessons sometimes have to be learned the hard way.

The whole Music Search Committee process was awful, and what made it worse was the committee was not successful in calling a minister of music. It is a complicated story, but simply put, after two long years of working to find the right minister of music for the church, our

Church Conflict: Not Mine to Do

candidate accepted our calling twice and then turned it down twice. We went before the church two times saying without a doubt this was the man for our church, only to stand in front of the congregation two more times and say essentially, "Just kidding. He's not coming." Exhausted, fractured, and humbled, the committee disbanded.

It is so easy to get lost in the nuts and bolts of church work. It is so easy to lose sight of what is most important: sharing Jesus and loving others. Grace for fellow members can evaporate as quickly as boiling water, and opposing views can make docile churchgoers steaming mad. The smoke can make it difficult to see the reality and truth of situations. Don't let arguments get in the way of the church's main goal and bigger picture. Aren't we on the same team? *(Lesson Four – As hard as it can be, try and rise above the noise and see things from God's perspective.)*

God's Perspective and Rising Above the Conflict

The topic of worship style was a line drawn on the sanctuary carpet. I hesitate to say this, but honestly, I never fully understood the debate. To all of my musical friends, please forgive me. I know intellectually, the value of music. I am often moved by music. The church of my youth was more liturgical in worship style, fitting neither the traditional nor contemporary requirements. I was as comfortable in "high" church with organ pipes blaring as I was in "low" church with my granny playing hymns by ear on an old upright piano or a loud band complete with drums and electric guitars.

One of the most profound worship experiences I have had was a funeral for a girl who died much too young. At her service, there were no musical instruments. Voices of all ages joined together in complex harmony. Hearts were raw and torn open as we searched for some meaning, some answers for this tragedy, but there would never be answers to the why. All we had was the understanding that we were passing through this life and living in the hope of an eternal home. We were united, not just in voice, but in our crying out to God to deliver us and be with us in our pain.

I have never sobbed so openly in public as I did during that service. I heard about a life well-lived. I heard about someone who impacted many in a very short amount of time. God was the focus, and Jesus was the hope. It was there, in that service, that I was drawn to the feet of Jesus. I vowed that day that this young life would not have lived in vain. I was a life changed by attending her funeral: a worship service.

While on the Music Search Committee, I lost sight of the true purpose of worship. Worship is when we give our deepest affection and highest praise to God. True worship of God is when we love Him with all our heart, soul, mind, and strength.

Differing Opinions and Common Ground

Is one person's way of worshipping right and another's wrong? I sure don't think so.

I was privileged to sit under the teaching and pastorship of Gary DeSalvo at Temple Bible Church in Temple, Texas. He used a phrase that has stayed with me through the years. When discussing "minor" issues of faith, such as worship styles, he would say that we might disagree on this, but we do not need to break fellowship over it. He meant that the topic of disagreement should not cause us to separate from one another. When possible, I will always be on the side of peace, compromise, and middle ground. Is there a way to come together, unified through the life and teachings of Christ? Three questions to ask when differing with fellow Christians in areas of faith or church: 1. Do we worship and pray to the same God? 2. Am I willing/needing to break fellowship with someone over this issue? 3. Do we share enough similar values to find common ground?

Peter, James (the brother of Christ), and Paul were three influential people who carried on the work of Jesus after His death and resurrection. They each played unique roles within the early church.

Church Conflict: Not Mine to Do

Peter was the leader of the church of Rome. James was the leader of the Jerusalem Church, and Paul was primarily a missionary. We know from our current vantage point that Peter, James, and Paul were the right men to carry on the work of Jesus. They, however, did not have our vantage point. They were learning as they went and often flying by the seat of their pants, or loincloth as the case may be. Paul, James, and Peter accepted the call to lead the early church. They had different backgrounds, experiences, and strengths to lead, teach, and discern how to begin this critical work that had never been done before! They knew what it was to teach in a synagogue and read the Torah, but this whole Christianity thing was brand new. They knew that God had called them to this work, but they didn't have all the answers before they started, and, not surprisingly, they each had their own ideas on how best to do things.

At the end of Acts 14, Paul and Barnabas gather the church together in Antioch. They are on an emotional and spiritual high returning from an amazing trip, "telling in great detail how God used them to throw the door of faith wide open so people of all nations could come streaming in" (Act 14: 27-28 Msg). I can feel their contagious enthusiasm and imagine they could not wait to get back out there and convert more and more believers. But as too often happens, other believers soon thwarted their joy, throwing a wet blanket on their fiery zeal. Not everyone catches on fire at the same time. Dissension, grumbling, doubt, and opposition can be smoldering right outside our doors, waiting for the right moment to ignite. The tiny sparks of doubt come knocking. You want to tell Paul and Barnabas not to open the door and add oxygen to the flames. The door, however, is forced open, and their enthusiasm combusts into ashes.

We learn where the opposition is coming from in Acts 15. There are Pharisees who have converted. Amazing! However, these Pharisees are not happy. No surprise! The Pharisees demand a council meeting. At the meeting, the Pharisees who are new converts, demand that Paul and Barnabas, "circumcise the pagan [gentile] converts. You must make them keep the Law of Moses" Act 15:5 (Msg). I think the term "pagan converts" gives insight into how far these men were from accepting Gentiles into the fold and embracing them as brothers in Christ.

James was a Jew, and his primary concern was with the mission of his people, the Jews. After Paul's conversion on the road to Damascus, Paul felt the Lord had made it clear that he was chosen to preach to the Gentiles (Acts 9:15). Acts records that the debates over Gentiles and Jewish law were heated and went long into the night, with arguments going back and forth. It is beautifully ironic that it is impulsive and opinionated Peter who steps up and stops the arguments. He stops the arguments by calling on all to remember their higher calling and to focus on the bigger picture. The Message Bible states that you could have heard a pin drop after Peter speaks. Listen to Peter's message that raises the council's focus above the conflict and encourages them to see the bigger picture:

> So why are you now trying to out-god God, loading these new believers down with rules that crushed our ancestors and crushed us too? Don't we believe that we are saved because the Master Jesus amazingly and out of sheer generosity moved to save us just as he did those from beyond our nation? So what are we arguing about? (Acts 15:10 MSG)

James and Paul had differing strategies to achieve the same goal. Of course they did! They had different views and ideas on encouraging and instructing new believers because of their backgrounds, unique relationship with Jesus, and their role in the church. Was one right and one wrong? At the time, their intentions were pure and good, but let's be honest, they didn't know what they were doing. It had never been done before! The idea of Christianity and the church was brand new. They were learning as they went. Of course, they would make mistakes and learn through trial and error, but both men ultimately were vital in spreading the gospel. Imagine if these men and their fellow workers had refused to act until they all agreed on how and what to do. They came to the same goal from different sides of the field. There were a few fumbles and missed field goals along the way, but listen, progress and growth are pretty much always clumsy and messy.

As believers, we sit across the table from someone who feels just as passionately as we do about the same issue but sees it completely different. Both perspectives may be needed to see a greater solution. The middle may be the end goal all along. Or, maybe the two views come together to develop a third option that hasn't yet been conceived. It's worth considering. We are better together. We are meant to be one body. Aren't we all on the same team? Sometimes, it may seem like we are high school rivals, but are our values and goals so different?

What about the times when the differences are too big and wide? What if our goals and values are vastly different? There really doesn't seem to be any common ground, and the person sitting across the table from you looks more like a stranger than a friend. What about when the person sitting next to you in the church pew seems more like an enemy than a brother or sister in Christ? Are there times when there is simply no possible resolution to the conflict? Is it ever necessary to end relationships over our differing viewpoints? Are there times when we need to break fellowship with one another?

Reflection/Discussion Questions

- What is your church history? Do you currently attend a church regularly? Why or why not?
- Are you someone who readily embraces change or resists change?
- How important are worship styles to you? When choosing a church, what are the most important criteria?
- Have you experienced conflict within a church? Was it handled well? Was a resolution reached?
- Are you comfortable with the idea of agreeing to disagree? What are the challenges that may come with adopting this idea?

- Have you had the experience of being able to rise above a conflict and been able to see things from God's perspective? How did His perspective change your perceptions of the situation?
- Have you ever been involved in a conflict only to wish later you had not been involved? Have you **not** been involved in a conflict only to wish later **you had** gotten involved?
- Do you have an example of a creative resolution to a conflict?

Chapter 12

Church Conflict: Taking a Stand

> Church hurt is confusing, concerning, and most often leaves hurting people isolated and unsure who to talk with to process their experience.[63]

IF YOU HAVE been a churchgoer for any length of time, you know the faces of a congregation change. Some people will stay at the same place of worship for many years, while others may attend many churches in their lifetime. My church membership has changed a few times in my life, but there has only been one time when the choice to leave was due to any type of conflict. It was one of the rare times I knew with certainty that it was my turn to take a stand against the majority and fall painfully on my sword. Though I don't wish this for anyone, there may be times we need to break fellowship with a church to remain true to our values and convictions.

How do we discern when it is time to break fellowship with a church due to differences of opinion or ideology and find a new place of worship? As stated a few times in this book, we each have varying thresholds regarding conflict tolerance. We also have differing ideas on the criteria of a healthy and Christ-centered church and what we deem an appropriate reason to change church membership. I entered

---

[63] Nate Brooks, "Why Won't My Feelings of Church Hurt Go Away," *Biblical Counseling Coalition*, (October 28, 2021) https://www.biblicalcounselingcoalition.org/2021/10/28/why-wont-my-feelings-of-church-hurt-go-away/

the question "What are the reasons to leave a church?" into my Google search engine, hoping for a quick and easy checklist, like an easy-to-follow guide on correct and proper etiquette for congregational exits. The articles I found were many. Similar answers were few. You might say the search results were directly contradictory or even conflictual.

The reasons found through my Google search ranged from wanting or needing different church programs to there being no acceptable reason ever for leaving a church. I started to compile a list of the most often stated reasons and then thought better of it. I am not creating a list of reasons to leave a church because I don't want to sway anyone one way or another. I want neither to sway someone to stay nor to encourage someone to leave. Deciding to change churches requires discernment, time, ongoing conversations between the people involved, and, most importantly, some heartfelt discussions with God.

We shouldn't be surprised by conflict within the Body of Christ. Scripture repeatedly instructs on preparing and dealing with such issues "when" they occur, not "if" they occur. Conflict within church bodies is inevitable. Why? We fight for what we care most about. We should be passionate about our faith and our church. It follows that emotions and opinions would be highly weighted regarding where, how, and with whom we worship.

Changing church membership or attendance is a reality of the American Christian life. I have seen it done well, and I have experienced it done poorly. How do you leave a church well? Is it possible to share your convictions with others without condemning or judging? Can you leave the institution of a particular church and not break fellowship with church members?

> Therefore, as God's chosen people, holy and dearly loved, clothe yourselves with compassion, kindness, humility, gentleness and patience. Bear with each other and forgive one another if any of you has a grievance against someone. Forgive as the Lord forgave you. And over all

> these virtues put on love, which binds them all together in perfect unity. Let the peace of Christ rule in your hearts, since as members of one body you were called to peace. And be thankful. (Colossians 3:12-15)

According to the above passage, it is possible to live well with others if we clothe ourselves in "compassion, kindness, humility, gentleness, and patience." Unfortunately, personal agendas, emotions, and baggage often hinder our execution of living like Christ. We hope that the church is above petty arguments and squabbles. Surely, of all places, the church should be free of discord! Oh, if only it were so. Our expectations of church unity may be unrealistically high. The church is made of people. It is hard enough to get a group to agree on where to go for lunch, much less how to love and serve the Lord your God with all your heart, soul, mind, and strength. As I've talked to people about church involvement, there is, most of the time, some kind of "church hurt." The very place where we should feel most loved and secure is often the place of greatest personal hurt because we have allowed our hearts to be open and vulnerable. It can be crushingly painful because we are wounded in the place where we most believe we should all agree all of the time.

> If you're reading this, it's safe to assume that something has either gone significantly wrong in your own church experience or in the lives of those to whom you minister. Church hurt is an inherently deadening topic, as it pierces right to the heart of the failures of God's people in one way or another. Church hurt is confusing, concerning, and most often leaves hurting people isolated and unsure who to talk with to process their experience.[64]

---

[64] Brooks, *Biblical Counseling Coalition*

And so, let's openly talk about it: breaking church fellowship. I have my own story of church hurt. It has taken years for the wounds to heal from the inside out. Some memory or casual remark no longer rips away the scabs, but the re-wounding and re-healing cycle lasted a very long time. At one point, I thought the wounds would never heal, but they did. God reached down in His loving and sovereign way and worked all things out for good. It ended up not just for my good, but for the greater good, the best for all.

I have said this before and will repeat it: people are messy and complex. They sometimes resemble a one-year-old learning to eat soup with a spoon for the first time, followed by a big piece of chocolate cake with thick dark chocolate frosting and no utensils. With our limited vision and clumsy emotions, we humans can make such a mess of things, but God can take our feeble fumbles and failings and somehow work them all together for good. "And we know that in all things God works for the good of those who love him, who have been called according to his purpose" (Romans 8:28). This doesn't mean that we come through life unscathed, far from it. The divine refining fire burns away the dross as we transform into Christ's likeness.

> These trials will show that your faith is genuine. It is being tested as fire tests and purifies gold—though your faith is far more precious than mere gold. So when your faith remains strong through many trials, it will bring you much praise and glory and honor on the day when Jesus Christ is revealed to the whole world. 1 Peter 1:7 (NIV)

Trials even occur in a place meant to be sacred. Some of my greatest refining has been due to conflict with fellow believers. The memories of my church hurt have faded, leaving only very faint scars and a complete restoration of relationships that have occurred through time and God's grace.

In this chapter, I am limiting the scope of "church hurt" to the conflict between church leaders and members. I am not referring to the still-painful experiences of arguments, disappointments, or disillusionments between members. We sinners make up the Body of Christ. We are all human and make mistakes. We must extend grace and forgiveness as we learn to live with our church family. In the next chapter, I specifically talk about conflict with individuals. The conflict discussed in the rest of this chapter pertains to repeated abuse of power by church leaders, resulting in conflict between leaders and members of the congregation.

My Story of Church Hurt

Almost 20 years ago, David and I found ourselves at a critical juncture in our relationship with our church. We were faced with knowledge of the inner workings of the church that we felt we couldn't ignore. Just to clarify, the offenses were not directed at us. The scope was much bigger than individual grievances or issues. There were repeated offenses by paid staff members that were damaging the foundation and fabric of our church. We could see the unraveling happening slowly. The frayed edges of what was once a strong tapestry of diverse and faithful people were being pulled apart by an invisible, frightening force that was difficult to discern. At times, we could sense something was wrong more than we could put our finger on specific events or situations that were causing the rift. It wasn't like a bear was chasing us, but more like we were being mocked by an elephant in the room. I have mentioned the aggressive and dangerous figurative bear we face when afraid or overwhelmed. This "bear" causes our defenses to go up and triggers our FFFF responses. The figurative elephant is a bit trickier. The proverbial elephant is an obvious problem or difficult situation, but people ignore it for convenience or comfort. Once in a while, some church members caught a glimpse of the figurative elephant hiding under a table or slowly rambling down the church halls. We weren't in immediate danger, except the elephant seemed to grow, and sightings of the still small creature became more frequent. It was much like the Heffalump from Winnie the Pooh. Was it real? It was so vague at times that I doubted myself. Was I imagining what was happening? Eventually, others confirmed there were indeed real problems within the church leadership. David and I had both seen it more than once. It was real. What were we to do? Do we remain silent, ignore what we know, or pull the curtain back and reveal what was happening? As it turns out, we did a little of both. We felt it was time to take a stand and go into battle; believe me, we were reluctant warriors. We did not come out unscathed. We fell on our swords for what we thought was the best for all. It hurt when no one else followed or trusted our stand. Ultimately, the conflict severed our ties with the church we loved. Our lives were never the same. We had nothing close to a victory but did what we thought was best for all. We felt we were true to our convictions and to God.

To Leave or Stay? That Was The Question

To say that my husband and I were heavily involved in the church would be a gross understatement. We both taught Sunday School, served on numerous committees, wrote and directed productions, delivered Angel Tree gifts at Christmas time, and much more. Our home was open to church-sanctioned gatherings of all kinds. We rarely missed Easter Sunday or Christmas Eve services because we had to be at church to lead or serve somewhere. Summers were spent teaching Vacation Bible School, sponsoring Youth Camps, leading Music Camps, and going on Mission trips. If a support group existed for overachieving church people, we would have been founding members. In retrospect, our involvement was a wee bit over the top. The people in the church were our community. They were our friends and chosen families. We raised kids together. We prayed together. We attended weddings and funerals together. We laughed and cried together. We thought we would be with these people forever. We were loyal to the people and the church's mission until we faced issues we could not ignore. There had been many other times of opposition and conflicting ideals within the church body, but this was not an issue that a church vote could resolve, nor could we continue to sweep the problems under the rug. Believe me when I say I wanted to sweep it away and hide it from sight, but it was too big and continued to grow. It was never our intention to leave this church. It was not something we had planned or had ever foreseen.

Issues arose within the church that we, as "insiders," were aware of that most of the congregation did not know. We were "insiders" only because of our leadership positions, and the meetings we attended allowed us to know some of the church's business that most were unaware of. We needed to be privy to certain information as lay leaders. It became apparent to David, me, and others that there were concerns with the integrity of some in church leadership. In our opinion, there was an abuse of power by more than one staff member. Decisions and actions against committee approval were problematic and made repeatedly. Small discrepancies and little white lies were tiny breadcrumbs regularly dropped in conversations and church meetings. When certain staff members were questioned about their behavior, there was no contrition or indication of intent to change. The manner in which criticism or instruction was received was defensive and dismissive. We were made to feel out of line if we questioned their authority or actions when, in fact, that was exactly what our positions and vantage points required according to the by-laws of our committee-led church. Committees were positioned to be the checks and balances of church business. Not all churches function this way, but this was the set and prescribed structure followed by this church. Numerous attempts were made to address situations openly and lovingly. We extended grace, then extended it again, and then a second, third, and fourth time. For months, we sat through meetings addressing various situations of broken church guidelines and growing falsehoods with no positive outcome. It became apparent that there was an abuse of power within the church leadership. The responses to shared concern with the staff became predictable and rigid. It was apparent that nothing was going to change. The staff members in question were not interested in finding solutions because they did not see themselves as part of the problem. They believed the problem was always someone else, and the finger-pointing also became part of their song and dance pattern. Arguments and incompatibilities within the staff were seeping out of the church offices, down the halls, and into the sanctuary. It became obvious that there was turmoil within the staff as many positions were vacated. The turnover of staff positions was numerous during this time, but the problems continued and seemed to have settled in for a long stay. It was a very real, significant, and concerning issue.

There was an increasing distrust of the people in charge. There was an unease about the spiritual leadership of the church. Sunday attendance ranged between 600 and 800 people, but attendance steadily decreased. Many attended Sunday school and other church functions but not Sunday morning worship services. Although there can be too much emphasis on church attendance and numbers, dwindling attendance and a lack of engagement of members can be a warning sign that something is amiss. The unwillingness of leadership to listen to anyone else for suggestions or solutions to problems is another red flag. Another concern is leadership that acts as if they are above reproach, dismissive of others, and unwilling to work with others. Finally, if someone constantly changes facts to fit their narrative or spins stories to manipulate outcomes, they do not have everyone's best interest. They are looking out more for their agendas and personal stories than what is best for the whole. We experienced all of these warnings and red flags more than once.

We increasingly knew there were big concerns, and it was steadily getting worse, but what do you do when the problem is the people to whom you would go to address the problem? They were the people in charge! Our position as church members and lay leaders was tricky because much of our information was confidential. We knew things that others did not know. We were not supposed to share things discussed in closed meetings with others. It also felt wrong to talk badly about people. It felt very unchristian to spread unpleasantness about anyone, especially our leaders!

Timothy Keller includes "reconciliation practices" in his book, "Forgiven." Galatians 6:1 states, "if someone is caught in a sin, you who live by the Spirit should restore that person gently."[65] Keller points out that if the motive is to restore the other person, then it will be done lovingly and gently. The word "stuck" in this verse indicates that someone has repetitive patterns of behavior. The reason for dealing with the situation is ultimately to restore the stuck person.

> Ultimately, any love that is afraid to confront the beloved is really not love but a selfish desire to *Be* loved. Cowardice is always selfish, putting your own needs ahead of the needs of the other. A love that says, "I'll do *anything* to keep him or her loving and approving of me!" is not real love at all. It is not loving the person – it is loving the love you get from the person. True love is willing to confront, even to "lose" the beloved in the short run if there is a chance to help him or her.[66]

It sounds so noble to say we wanted to bring restoration to the church. We didn't feel noble. We felt scared. We were scared to act and scared not to act. At this point, no decision was making a decision. No action was deciding upon an action. Silence at this point would make us complicit.

The inner circle of committee and staff members were privy to knowledge of repeated violations and character issues, but not most of the congregation. So, for us, it became the elephant in the room. What we deemed questionable behavior by paid leaders was HUGE and

---

[65] Timothy Keller, *Forgive: Why Should I and How Can I?* (New York, Viking an imprint of Penguin Random House, 2022) 218

[66] Keller, *Forgive: Why Should I and How Can I?*, 218

obvious. In retrospect, the rest of the church was mostly oblivious to the issues because the grievances were not widely known. It was hard to believe others did not see what was happening then. We were seeing evidence of bad behavior almost weekly. The problems consumed us. We were burdened and concerned for the future of the church. It was a dark and unsettling time. We kept what we knew a secret from most, not wanting to be divisive or gossip, taking seriously that we were to edify the body and encourage one another (Eph. 4:12). It felt dirty and underhanded to keep this information from others. We not only kept the secrets to avoid division within the church, but we also did not want to hurt family members and friends of the staff. Our intentions were good if handling the situation often felt wrong and clumsy. Discernment of transparency is difficult. We ultimately did what we thought was best for the greater good.

I talked to people who were "in the know" of the behind-the-scenes workings of the church. I found many relieved to have someone to vent to, finally able to talk freely about their concerns. Others did not share the concern or agree with the severity of staff members not adhering to church by-laws or following procedures set forth by the committee-led church. There was a sense that we were overreacting. My journal during these days is filled with questioning my motives and judgments. Was I wrong? Was I overreacting? Was I trying to create drama where there was none? Do I need to be quiet and extend grace and mercy no matter the outcome?

"Too often we fixate on our disagreements, and we feel like we can't worship with such a big elephant in the room. We don't see that God is infinitely larger than our elephants."[67] I tried to rise above the conflict. I really did. I so wanted to rise above it and float along the blissful river of denial. I prayed alone and with others. I prayed that God would either change me or them or miraculously keep me from seeing that ugly elephant in the middle of the sanctuary. I was told that we (church

---

[67] Chan, *Until Unity*, 113

members) were the church and would be there long after staff members were gone. In other words, "this too shall pass." Just hang on and wait. We waited. And we waited some more. Nothing changed.

Now, I will be the first to tell you that if you are the only one who sees a problem, chances are there isn't a problem, or the problem may just be you. Right? But others saw the issues and either weren't ready to deal with them or hadn't experienced them to the extent we had. We saw and experienced things that went against our core values, and we felt they went against the life and teachings of Jesus. We all sin and should extend grace and forgiveness to those who repent, but their pattern of behavior never changed and seemed to intensify as personal agendas were blocked. What do we do? Stay and bury our heads in the sand? Ignore what was happening? Turn a blind eye? Stay and continue to beat our heads against a wall, knowing change was unlikely? History has too many examples of people looking the other way instead of standing on their convictions and principles. It was time to leave if we weren't heard and no one was willing to take action.

In the spring, before my youngest daughter was old enough to finally cross the parking lot and enter the sacred and mysterious youth building she had longed to enter her whole life, David and I decided to leave our church. I remember the timing of the decision well because our daughter made sure we knew for many years how devasted she was to never be part of this particular youth group. Ah, a mother's guilt is real and strong!

David and I both decided to leave internally without discussing it directly with each other. On the way home after a particularly disturbing Sunday morning, with our unsuspecting kids in the backseat, we looked at each other and said, "It's time to leave." Our conviction, individually and as a couple, confirmed this was the right decision. We knew this was the right thing for us to do, not just for us but for our young teenage girls. All these years later, I still say we made the right decision for our little family of four. It was an extremely difficult decision. We were bruised and defeated. We were setting out on our own without knowing what the future held. And our children were less than happy about it. They were mad and hurt from being unwillingly yanked from their church home.

As we drove away one last time, through the old stained-glass windows, I could see the still small but growing elephant jumping up and down on the pews and laughing at us, waving his trunk goodbye mockingly. Little did we know that the elephant would continue to grow until its body's weight strained the church's very foundation.

The Fallout of Leaving

It is hard for me to remember the chain of events accurately. Many years have passed, and I know memories are not always accurate. I do remember that our quiet leaving was loudly heard, and rumors spread quickly about why we left. One rumor about our departure was that we didn't like the church's worship style. To understand how absurd this was to me, read the prior chapter. What hurt me the most was I knew the person spreading this rumor and was dismayed that they would ever think me so shallow. To think that someone who knew me so well would say that I would leave the church body that I loved and cared so much about because of a style of singing stung badly. Another person I respected immensely told me she was saddened that I was no longer using my spiritual gifts. She meant she was sad I wasn't using my gifts in *her* church. She didn't even ask me what I was doing or if I was serving elsewhere. I wasn't serving with and for her, so in her eyes, I wasn't serving.

I was unprepared for the loss of friendships and relationships. I thought the deep relational bonds went beyond the church walls and would remain. I thought we would continue to be a part of each other's lives. We were so much more than just Sunday morning acquaintances. We were family! Or so I thought. We lived in a small town; the church had been our whole community. The circles we ran in were so small that we could not just fade into the masses. Our lives remained interconnected whether we wanted it or not. Once we left, it felt like our club membership was revoked, and we were no longer welcome. We were excluded from the inclusion of people's lives overnight.

> Nearly every member who has left our local church has said something like, "We want to stay in touch… we will also visit on occasion." Sometimes they try for a while, but it is simply not possible to stay involved with two different churches.
> A local church is very much like a family. Within that family many joys are shared like marriages, childbirth, graduations, etc. Likewise, when family members depart, hearts are broken and relationships are permanently altered.
> By all means, stay in touch with old friends if you can, but do not expect that your departure will leave such relationships unchanged.
> This is one of the many costs which needs to be counted while considering the question, "Should I leave my church?"[68]

We were given cold shoulders at the grocery store and sporting events. And then, on top of that, we endured ongoing criticism for leaving the church, even by those who knew the real reason for our exit. "What is happening?" I wondered. It felt like I was in some badly written science fiction movie. I couldn't follow the plot and no longer recognized the once-familiar characters. I kept thinking, "We are the ones who have sacrificed everything to do what we felt was right. You all still have each other. What is the big deal? You all have lost nothing."

---

[68] Christian McShaffrey, "Leaving a Church to the Glory of God," *Reformation 21*, (May 26, 2021) https://www.reformation21.org/blog/leaving-a-church-to-the-glory-of-god

I was hurt by the lies spread about us. The distrust of our motives, especially by those who knew us well, angered me. I felt like the church had used us, and once we could no longer serve it, we were spat out and forgotten. We lost not only our packed social calendar but we lost our support group. We lost friendships. We were no longer invited to weddings and seemed to miss any notifications about illnesses or funerals. Later, I learned we had been removed from email communications and, therefore, would learn of someone's death long after the fact. These were people I thought would be my forever family in Christ. I could not fathom why we were shunned and cast out. These people knew us. They knew our hearts. We had sacrificed and given so much of ourselves to this church body gladly and willingly for over ten years. I was in so much emotional pain it was hard to know which way was up or down or if I was coming or going. It felt like we were on a small boat drifting in a stormy ocean with no shore in sight.

It didn't take me long before the responses to our leaving made me mad. How dare they treat me and my family this way!! I felt attacked. My defenses went up just as if a bear were chasing me with teeth bared and claws out, and all I had to defend myself with were toxic words. I flipped my lid, and my FFFF responses went into overdrive. **WE** were the ones that were courageous and right to leave. **THEY** were cowards and wrong to deny what was happening within the church. Just Like that, I entered the dangerous and destructive territory of **US** vs. **THEM**.

> Rejection is especially debilitating when it blindsides us… In experiments, people who expect acceptance and encounter rejection instead tend to react with more hostility. That's because threats that are unexpected and unpredictable feel more dangerous to us…In study after study, ostracized people typically respond that way. First, they try to win back the affection of others. They hasten to conform and comply (or try to). If that doesn't work, they become aggressive.

> And people who feel disrespected…respond with even more aggression than people who simply feel disliked.[69]

I wish with all my heart that I handled the fallout gracefully. Some days, I did better than others, sitting like a duck in a cold and lonely pond, allowing the hurtful comments and quiet shaming to roll off my back. Other times, I did my own share of shaming and blaming. As in most cases, what was needed was time and perspective for all to understand the issue's complexity. It was not a simple problem, and at the time, it felt like it was too great ever to overcome.

Beauty from Ashes

Our little family of four limped into another church and began a long healing process. All these years later, we know we would still make the same decision to leave. It was the right decision for us, but I now acknowledge that as much courage as it took to leave, I am so glad others dared to endure and stay. All these years later, I can see how God worked all of this together in a complicated and beautiful way. I wish I had known fully what I know now. It is possible to stand and kneel at the same time. I had to put down a lot of baggage before my hands were free to receive and extend grace.

> My only challenge was learning how to receive anger and not give it back in return. I needed to do something very difficult: to stand and kneel at the same time. I needed to stand in my conviction, laying out what I believed and why. And when the response was anger, I needed to learn to kneel before it. Believe me self-righteousness is so much easier. But when you're facing someone else who feels as strongly in their conviction as you do, anger is totally unproductive. Actually, it's counterproductive.

---

[69] Ripley, *High Conflict*, 72

> You've got to create space for the other person…This isn't easy, and it's even harder if the anger is coming at you from people you love and cherish, rather than strangers.[70]

People slowly left the church for the next five to six years. I don't know if you asked people if they would share similar reasons for leaving. There was an unease and a sense throughout the church that all was not right. The people leaving were active members. Again, this was a small town, so it was noticeable when one left a church and started attending another. I believe that the "elephant" staked out his claim in the church building and grew and grew until the pressure on the church walls could no longer hold. Something had to release the pressure, and something did.

On January 19, 2010, a fire destroyed the 70-year-old church building, leaving nothing but rubble and ash. There was evidence the fire was deliberately set, but the guilty party was never apprehended. The beautiful stained-glass windows were all blown out by the pressure built up inside the building. There was so much lost due to the fire: wooden pews, pipe organ, choir robes, office equipment, documents, music, scripts, Easter pageant costumes, chandeliers, and the baptistry I gazed at so many Sundays.

I know that the figurative elephant my imagination conjured up didn't truly have anything to do with the fire. The fire was man-made, but so was the elephant. It was man-made, and the cost was so very high. Man was at fault for creating the sparks that started the fire. Man was at fault for not ushering the elephant out of the building. But God was victorious in accomplishing what man could not. What man intended for devastation, God used to refine and purge. Beauty truly does come from ashes.

The old guard, the faithful who had stayed when so many had left, gathered around the burning inferno and watched what they knew of their church building disappear. They knew the building was ultimately not their church. It was just brick and mortar. Over time, the congregation

---

[70] Curry, *Love is The Way*, 181-182

agreed that the fire had opened the door for big changes. Together, the church rolled up its sleeves and got to work. It is good to remember that your home church is a building whose name most likely includes the word "Church" spelled with a capital "C." But, all believers are part of His church, spelled with a little "c," and His church cannot be destroyed or pulled apart by fire, man, or elephant.

> Changing doesn't mean simply doing something different. Changing involves a willing spirit, a new thought, and plenty of backbone. Changing can mean sloughing off our past like an old skin, so old stories no longer define us. And some of those old stories were written for us before we even knew how to write. We can determine the truth or lies that wrote those old stories. We can close the chapter on the stories that don't help us anymore. Experiencing the freedom of new understanding and knowledge makes the past bearable, and sometimes we can even celebrate its lesson.[71]

Land was purchased, staff changed, and the congregation met for their first service in a new church building four years after the fire.

> The whole church had an identity in a gorgeous new building God had made available. Sunday worships services and Life group attendance grew. Worship services expanded from the original two to four before the end of 2014. The number of children attending church reflected the influx of young families streaming into the church.[72]

Today, the church is growing and vibrant. Time and intention have healed fractured relationships. We attend weddings and funerals

---

[71] Stevens, *Practically Divine*, 71

[72] Thomas David Yeilding, *Through Wind and Fire: A History of First Baptist Church Temple, Texas*, (2019) 232

together. We laugh fondly at shared memories. I regularly see many friends from that era of life. They are my tried-and-true friends. We've actually been through a fire together. About half of them stayed at the church, and about half left. And guess what? I love and respect each of them. Time and God's grace have healed us. We may not all be in the same building, but we still worship the same God. God is the same, and God is good. He is the King of Restoration.

Reflection/Discussion Questions

- Name one thing from this chapter that troubled you, encouraged you, or both. Why were you impacted in this way?
- Do you have a personal story of church hurt? What was the situation? Have you been able to discern the root cause of the hurt? How was the situation handled or resolved?
- How would you have handled the situation after hearing Kristy's conflict at her church? What would you have done differently? Have you ever had to deal with an "elephant in the room?"
- Have you ever experienced a time when your motives were misunderstood? Have you ever experienced persecution? If so, describe the experience. How did it impact your relationship with Christ? With other people?
- Have you experienced others leaving your church? How did it impact you? Did you ask the person(s) why they were leaving? Why or why not?

Chapter 13

Church Conflict–Lessons Learned

Even though your brain works at lightening-fast speed, it's easy to imagine hours, months, or even years of argument among three members of your brain committee about whether you should stay or go, comply or protest, confess or deny, speak or remain silent. Your head might tell you to go or speak, you heart might tell you to stay or remain silent, while your gut may be torn between the two.[73]

Returning to the metaphor of our lives being like a garden, it makes sense that we each arrive at different opinions and conclusions at different times. We each have experiences, beliefs, and priorities planted with deep, intricate root systems that are difficult to dig up and change. When faced with a new situation or idea, people tend to try to make new thoughts fit into their already set thinking patterns. It is much more comfortable to prune ideas to fit your old ideals, even if the facts do not logically support the old way of thinking. Confirmation bias is "the human tendency to interpret new information as confirmation of one's preexisting beliefs."[74]

---

[73] Brian D. McLaren, *Faith After Doubt: Why Your Beliefs Stopped Working and What to Do About It*, (New York, St. Martin's Essentials, 2021) 18

[74] Ripley, *High Conflict*, Glossary

There is No Bear. Just Breathe.

> A mind is more like a pile of millions of little rocks than a single big boulder. To change a mind, we need to carry thousands of little rocks from one pile to another, one at a time. This is because our brains don't know how to rewire a full belief in one big haul. New neuron paths aren't created that quickly. You might be able to get a tiny percent of someone's mind to rewire to a new belief in a given conversation, but minds change slowly and in unpredictable ways.[75]

As strongly as we felt the need to leave the church, there were others who felt just as strongly the need to stay. The church was like a chosen family. Many believed you were loyal to your family no matter what. You didn't bail ship on family. You stayed. Some stayed and continued to actively work toward positive change. So, which side was right and which was wrong?

I cringe at how certain I once was of my rightness, like the church lady in a Saturday Night Live skit, painfully smug and pious and equally repulsive. I often dug my heels in to defend something I was sure to be true, only to find out it wasn't exactly what I thought it was. My view just didn't hold water; my arguments had more holes in them than my grandmother's sieve. Or I didn't have all the facts. Or maybe, just maybe, there wasn't a right or wrong.

Many of my convictions have changed over the years. Evolving views happen, don't they? Life experiences can push us to a new space, allowing us to see new angles and intersections. I once held opinions tightly, gripping them like a child holding on to a fast, whirling merry-go-round. If I were to let go, I would be flung into the air, not knowing where I would land, certainly not knowing if I would land safely. I hold opinions more loosely now. I recognize how malleable our thoughts and ideas are. Shifting and changing our minds and hearts

---

[75] Benson, *Why Are We Yelling*, 19

can be challenging, scary, and uncomfortable, but growth is impossible without change. In planting, a seed must die for the plant to grow. A caterpillar's old body must die before a butterfly can be born. Old ideals and ideas must die before we are transformed more and more into the likeness of Christ.

> Dear Reader, here is what I'm thinking right now – but would you forgive me and not hold it against the God of whom I speak if time or divine Providence proves me wrong or woefully deficient?[76]

Sometimes, we have to take the first step before we have a clear view of the path in front of us. We fight for the things we care about. We fight for those we love. We fight for love, but can we fight with love? Can those two things truly go together? Fighting and loving?

How Do You Eat an Elephant?

I wanted a resolution to the conflict between those who chose to stay at the church and those who chose to leave. I mean, I badly wanted a resolution. I could not let it go. My mind dwelt on all the thoughts and feelings surrounding the conflict. All of the what-ifs and what could have been. I had a loop playing non-stop in my brain about past hurts and ways I thought I had been wronged. The need for validation was so strong. Please tell me I'm not the only person that has felt this way. It turns out that we humans have great difficulty leaving things unresolved. Phew!

> Discomfort is key to our growth, and desirable. Anxiety is key to our growth, and desirable. What is all this discomfort and anxiety about, anyway? It's about wanting to

---
[76] Moore, *All My Knotted Up Life*, 2

> have the answer, wanting to solve the problem. *Wanting it to go away.* To remove everything that's wrong and replace it with things that are right. To replace bad with good. To solve the mystery. To yang the yin. To escape the threat. To close the loop. To resolve the disagreement. This desire to close the loop is embedded deep within our psychology.
> ….This dynamic between tension and release that makes us laugh at jokes, dance to music, and get out of bed every morning to see what the day has in store for us is the same mechanism that makes it really difficult for us to sit with something that's unresolved. It's incredibly uncomfortable.[77]

I wanted to be released from these consuming thoughts and feelings. I was sick and tired of my unexplained need to keep digging up the past and gnawing at it like a dog with a bone. But how could I let it go? Just telling myself to stop was not working. I wanted validation and needed to be right, but I also knew there would never be some kind of epiphany or mass "a-ha" moment for which I longed.

When our opinion differs from someone else, we often feel it is just a matter of sharing our viewpoint, and the other person will instantly and magically change their mind. We have seen movies where whole groups of people suddenly see the truth of a situation, and the protagonist is either publicly declared a hero or has the silent satisfaction of knowing he or she has saved people from their delusion. In reality, this rarely happens. Changing minds is most often a very slow process. Instead of one huge shift in thinking, changing one's mind is many tiny shifts that happen gradually. One new thought causes other preconceived ideas to shift. It can take many shifts before a belief is completely released.

---

[77] Benson, *Why Are We Yelling*, 107

Church Conflict–Lessons Learned

There is an old adage: How do you eat an elephant? The answer: One bite at a time.

I was stuck in a destructive cycle and could not find my way out. Instead of eating the elephant, I allowed the situation to consume me. It was eating *me* alive. Anytime you refer to a group as "those people," it is time to step back and examine what is underneath those words. At the time, I was so hurt I couldn't see straight. Both sides, "us and them," were hurting, and hurting people hurt people. We had each gone through a painful "divorce" of sorts. David and I were the ones who filed the papers and were looking outside of the current relationship for something new. We felt misunderstood. Our motives were harshly criticized. We didn't feel right in spreading disparaging information about the church, but that's what "they" were doing to "us."

Why did I see people who were responding differently than me as the enemy? When you start to see "us vs. them", "right vs. wrong," or good vs. evil, it is time to step back and re-evaluate. In Amanda Ripley's book, *High Conflict*, she asks a series of questions to determine if the reader is involved in what she terms high conflict: "A conflict that becomes self-perpetuating and all-consuming, in which almost everyone ends up worse off. Typically an us-versus-them conflict."[78] Here are a few of the questions she asks.

1. Do you lose sleep thinking about this conflict?
2. Do you feel good when something bad happens to the other person or side, even if it doesn't directly benefit you?
3. If the other side were to do something you actually agreed with, some small act, would it feel very uncomfortable to acknowledge this out loud?
4. Does it feel like the other side is brainwashed, like a cult member, beyond the reach of moral reasoning?

---

[78] Ripley, *High Conflict*, 286

5. Do you ever feel stuck? Like your brain keeps spinning, ruminating over the same grievances over and over again, without ever uncovering any new insights?
6. When you talk about the conflict with people that agree with you, do you say the same things over and over – and leave the conversation feeling slightly worse than when you started talking?[79]

It is easy to get stuck in the cycle of high conflict. The definition given states that it is "self-perpetuation and all-consuming" and that "everyone ends up worse off." It is not constructive and can ultimately lead to unproductive thinking, destructive behavior, and broken relationships. I knew I had to break fellowship with the institution of a particular church, but I did not want to lose relationships. It took years before many relationships were healed. Here are a few things I've learned and wished I'd done differently now that I have a better understanding of high conflict.

Breaking the Cycle of High Conflict

1. Personal Excavation: Examine yourself and your motives before criticizing the speck in someone else's eye. Make sure you've checked to see if there is a log in yours. Chapters two through five of this book contain what I hope will be helpful questions and practical exercises for self-examination.

Scott Sauls's book, "A Gentle Answer," shares the story of when Jesus told the twelve disciples that one of them would betray him. I have had some fun with the actions and reactions of the disciples in this book, but this story reflects the personal and transformational growth of these men as a result of their time with Jesus. Their responses were

---

[79] Ripley, *High Conflict*, 286

not to point fingers at each other, but instead, they each asked, "Is it I?" (Mark 14:19)

> This "Is it I?" response to the Lord, as opposed to an "It is he!" response, is a key indicator of a healthy, self-aware, non-presumptuous, gentle posture of faith. Sorrow mixed with introspection is, even for the most faithful disciples among us, the most appropriate response when the subject of evil and betrayal is raised. For none of us has measured up to the standard of true faithfulness. And all of us 'have sinned and fall short of the glory of God"(Rom. 3:23). The more we realize these truths, the less accusatory we will become toward others, and the gentler we will become as well.[80]

2. Recognize and honor the complexity of the issue or situation in which you find yourself. Slow down. Take the time needed to understand the whole story. Conflict is rarely simple or binary. There are rarely only two sides to a story. Most conflict is nuanced and multi-layered.
3. Dig for the understory. What is really going on underneath the words and behavior?

When I think back to the story of leaving a church, I recall that we felt bereft and alone. We were afraid. We feared isolation and lack of support. There were more questions than answers. Would we ever have the same type of community? Who would help us if we needed it? Our whole world was turned upside down, and on top of that, our children were not happy about leaving their home church. Not at all! It is no wonder that I lashed out. I was afraid. I had lost so much, and the hurt was so deep. Had I recognized how deeply hurt I was, and

---

[80] Sauls, *A Gentle Answer*, 164

acknowledged these emotions were not wrong but an indication of some areas that I needed healing in my own life, my interactions with others would have gone so much better. This was my understory, but I was so caught up in my own pain, I had not tried to truly understand the other side's point of view.

What about the other side? The ones left behind? What was their hurt? It took me a long time to fully understand what they were experiencing. Have you ever been left behind? Have your best friends moved to another town? Have you ever had a season of profound loss of one kind or another? Their loss was significant and unsettling. We left them. We deserted them. We chose to leave them. We may just as well have screamed at them that we didn't love them anymore. Our departure left a void. The vacancy we left was scary and significant for some. Who would step up and fill the empty holes?

For the people who knew of the unethical behavior in the church, our leaving felt like a judgment on their staying. If we felt right to leave, then, therefore, they were wrong to stay. Understand, that is not the way we felt at all. Because we were not open and honest about the reasons for our departure, some let their imaginations take over as to why we might have left. This caused an unease of suspicion of what was wrong with their church, which, in turn, made people defensive. They were afraid and unsettled. It is no wonder that they were trying to fill in the gaps and make sense of disconcerting decisions being made by others.

Try to distance yourself and see the bigger picture. What is the whole story? What is the understory?

4. Be curious. Ask questions. It is interesting how few people asked us why we left. Avoid leading questions that sound like accusations. Try to remain neutral. The questions are not meant to get the other person to see your point of view. Genuinely be curious about what they are thinking or feeling. Try to put emotions aside, and when emotions become too intense, take a break. If you ask questions, the other person will most likely

become curious about your views, and honest communication can begin.
5. Listen to the other person and be respectful of everything they share. Repeating what they say to you is helpful to ensure you have heard them correctly.
6. Check your motivation. Let go of the need to be right. As difficult as it may be to accept, the conflict may never be tied up with a beautiful, neat, and shiny bow. Ask yourself if this is something you can agree to disagree on. Can you accept that there may never be a resolution? If not, why?
7. Extend grace to others and to yourself. Pray for forgiveness for yourself and extend it to others. These can be a messy and awkward exchanges, but it is necessary if we are to live in a healthy community with others.
8. Take a break from the situation to gain a better perspective if needed. This could be an hour, weeks, or longer. If you don't have the luxury of time, enlist confidants to be your sounding board or audience before you talk to others directly involved in the conflict. Saying what we are thinking aloud can help us to hear ourselves. Bringing our thoughts into light by speaking them instead of hiding them in our dark, swirling brains can help clarify our thinking. Ideas can sound stronger in our heads but weaken once they are spoken out loud.
9. Find common ground. If these are people you've liked and respected up to this point, they haven't changed. You haven't changed. You just see something differently. Remember what it is that you liked about this person. Talk about common interests, even if it is just coffee or hobbies. Remembering or finding commonality helps us see the human being on the other side of an issue instead of just an opponent or foe.

Conflict is not something to fear. Through the writing of this book, I have realized so many unpleasant situations could have been avoided by having honest and constructive discussions. I would have never intentionally opened a space for disagreement. I now see all of the benefits of talking, listening, sharing ideas, open to change. Ask questions! What is the other person(s) thinking? Talk about the elephant in the room. What is the question, the real question, that no one is asking? What do you need the "other side" to know?

Have the courage to have the hard conversations before leaving a church, organization, or institution. It will be difficult and uncomfortable, but if at all possible, let someone know of your reasons. Once you've made your decision to leave, it is best to talk directly to the other person or group that is causing your leaving. Go to someone in charge so that documentation or a record of your grievances can be made. It may not help or feel good in the moment, but it may help resolve future conflicts and ultimately be critically important for the people left behind.

Reflection/Discussion Questions:

- Have you ever tried to change someone's mind recently? How did it go? Can you relate to the idea of digging up someone's garden or exchanging a pile of rocks with someone? Can you come up with another image to describe how it feels to face someone with a different viewpoint?
- Have you ever been stuck in a High Conflict cycle? How were you able to get out of it or are you still in it?
- Look through the nine ideas given for breaking the conflict cycle. Is there one that is harder for you than others? Do you have examples of any of the nine suggestions given?

Chapter 14

Conflict with Friends, Family, and God

Dr. John Gottman says that a relationship without conflict is a relationship without communication and is bound to fail. Conflict is inevitable whenever two or more people are talking about things from their own perspectives. Disagreements are a sign that the relationship's soil is healthy.[81]

"IT IS BETTER to have loved and lost than to never have loved at all." This sounds poetic and beautiful until you are in a relationship that hits a bump in the road. We've discussed unintentional conflict, the conflict that unsuspectingly finds us. We've talked about the conflict we knowingly choose to enter. We touched on conflict within the institution of the church, but what about those uncomfortable squabbles between people? Not strangers, but our friends and family? What happens when you go toe to toe with an individual you like? Someone you know well. The two of you have found yourself on opposite sides of an issue, and neither seems ready to change their stance any time soon. What then?

The quote by Dr. Gottman at the beginning of this chapter states that reasonable conflict is a sign of a healthy relationship. Sharing our opinions and perspectives with others we know is part of having close relationships. Without honest sharing, we are nothing but the shells

---

[81] Benson, *Why are We Yelling*, 8

of ourselves. The relationship is a façade with no substance. Do you have anyone in your life that when around them you must be guarded in what you say or do? It's just easier to tip-toe around them so as not to evoke their wrath or criticism. It kind of feels like you stepped onto the set of *Stepford Wives*, where everyone is just a little too perfect and plastic. Some people we know are not in our safe bubble. They have not been invited in through our figurative garden gate. It is not only good to have boundaries with these people, it is wise, but what about the people we do feel safe with? Those people we enjoy being around and would say they are in our inner circle. What happens if we have topics on which we strongly disagree?

We will have differing opinions, and that is okay. In fact, it's better than okay. Healthy differences keep us from stagnating or becoming rigid and unyielding. Disagreements may be uncomfortable, but they can be a sign of healthy relationships. It's not disagreeing with someone that can cause problems but how we handle the disagreement.

I hate to be the one to break it to you, but you will never find someone who agrees with you on every issue. It's just not going to happen. If you think you do have this relationship, someone is not being honest. And, really, do you want someone to always agree with you? Growth comes from opening ourselves up to new thoughts and ideas. Iron sharpens iron. There are times, however, when the sharpening process can inflict a few nicks and cuts. What are some things to remember when we find ourselves in a healthy discussion or debate with someone we care about?

1. As always, start with yourself. Are you in a good mental, emotional, and physical state for this discussion? If you're hangry maybe it's best to wait until you are fed and rested before entering this debate.
2. If you feel your emotions take over, take a break. If this is someone you know well, it's perfectly acceptable to say, "let me think about this and get back to you" or be more honest and

direct and say, "I can tell I'm getting too emotional. I need a break." If you say you will return to the discussion, you need to return to it. It is better to admit to needing time and space than to say or do something you will regret.
3. You don't have to continue in a discussion if it is something you feel is best to leave alone. Our family has adopted a saying: "We don't have a pony in the race." This is something we know doesn't warrant our direct involvement. Maybe we don't have all the facts needed, or we don't know all the players involved in the dispute. Whatever the reasons, we don't feel we must be directly involved in the conflict.
4. Listen to the other person's point of view. This is how we learn, grow, and change. Repeat back to them what they are saying so that you can be sure you have a clear understanding of what they are saying.
5. If you need help understanding their point of view, ask questions. Be curious about how they see the situation or information. What is their understory on this topic?
6. Be willing to agree to disagree. You may need to be the one who changes the subject or interrupts the debate. Very few disagreements are worth ending a good, solid relationship. In the previous chapter, I brought up my need for a resolution between church members staying or leaving. There is a human tendency to want to wrap up everything in a nice, neat little package. Sometimes, it is hard to let an argument go. We get wrapped up in the need to be right and prove the other person wrong. Is proving you're right worth the ending of a friendship?

Breaking Fellowship with an Individual

Are there times when a disagreement crosses a line, and there needs to be a break in fellowship with an individual? Relational endings happen for various reasons: a move causing geographical separation, schedule changes causing time limitations, or new interests causing a change of priorities. Relationships change. It is a fact of life. Few relationships will stay for a lifetime. Life circumstances will inevitably cause a natural and gradual separation from various people. These changes do not occur due to conflict between people. The changes happen over time, and neither party is hurt or offended. The widely accepted theory is that most friendships don't last past seven years. If your relationship makes it past seven years chances are it will last a long time, maybe even a lifetime.

Unlike family, you get to choose your friends and so you also get to choose to lose your friends. Though it may be painful, not all of our friendships remain viable and healthy long-term. What happens when a relationship becomes destructive? The bad times far outweigh the good times. What are the signs we may need to distance ourselves from someone? In Nedra Glover Tawwab's, *The Set Boundaries Workbook*, she has a checklist for the signs of an unhealthy friendship.[82]

- The relationship is competitive.
- You exhibit your worst behavior when you're with your friend.
- You feel emotionally drained after connecting with your friend.
- Your friend tries to embarrass you in front of others.
- You don't have anything in common.
- Your friend shares details of your personal life with others.
- The friendship is not reciprocal (i.e., you give more than you receive.)
- You're unable to work through disagreements.
- Your friend doesn't respect your boundaries.
- The relationship is enmeshed or codependent.

One of the criteria given above is the inability to work through disagreements. If you deem this friendship healthy outside of one or two

---

[82] Tawwab, *The Set Boundaries Workbook*, 160

topics, you might need to set some boundaries with the person. You and your friend(s) may decide certain topics need to be off-limits. All agree this is not something you will talk about. I know friends who have chosen not to talk about food choices. One is a strict vegetarian based on moral convictions, while the other believes man's ability to eat both meat and vegetables is a gift from God. The two will never agree on this, but their relationship is more important than needing to be right. I know another set of friends who worked together for years. At one point, there was a conflict at work that was heated and divisive. The two long-time friends found themselves on opposite sides of an issue. To this day, I don't know what the work issue entailed because they do not talk about it. They are still great friends because they respect this boundary. Unfortunately, some may not be able to adhere to the set boundaries.

> Relationships are wonderful until they're not…All relationships can be difficult at times, but they should not be destructive to our well-being…Drawing boundaries can help put out fires before they are all consuming. But if the fire keeps burning with increasing intensity, you've got to get away from the smoke and flames. Sometimes, your only option is to say goodbye.[83]

The unique thing about friendships is that these are people you have chosen to be in your life, so you can choose to exclude them from your life. The decision is yours, but it is one I suggest you put lots of thought into before ending or changing any relationship. Be careful about ending friendships. There can be repercussions, anger, and hurt if you don't handle it right. How will the decision impact other people? Are you part of a friend group? Will changing your relationship with one friend affect the other people in the group? What about kids and

---

[83] Lysa Terkeurst, *Good Boundaries and Goodbyes: Loving Others without Losing the Best of Who You Are*, (Nashville, Tennessee, Nelson Books, 2022) 6-7

spouses? Was this a family friend? Imagine your life without this person. How does it make you feel if they were no longer in your life?

There are many books written and advice given on how to end romantic relationships, but not many on how to end platonic relationships. I have always believed a slow change in the amount of time spent with someone would gradually change the dynamics of a friendship. I believe it is best not to burn bridges unless absolutely necessary. I would never come out and tell someone that I just didn't like them anymore. How awful would that be for both parties? And then what happens if you see that person again? How awkward! But I have also experienced those relationships where I've been the one ghosted, or I can tell the other person is distancing themselves from me. That kind of ending can be painful as well. Is it better to pull a band aid off slowly or quickly? A provocatively entitled book *How to Break Up with Your Friends* discusses friendships at length, including what to do when your friendship expiration date seems to have come and gone. The author, Erin Falconer, challenged me to think in new ways about how to end relationships.

> Does the relationship demand an explicit conversation? It's one thing to allow a workplace friendship to slowly cool without explanation, but it we're talking about someone you've known well for years, you should honor that relationship with a conversation. Or a letter. Or an email. Being direct with a person, even though you might have lost that warm and fuzzy feeling, allows you to still pay respect to the institution of friendship and to the better times you did have with the other person. This is a really difficult thing to do, and upon even thinking about it, a thousand excuses will flood your mind. Take the time to weed out real reasons not to do it versus your own anxiety and fear of talking about it.[84]

---

[84] Erin Falconer, *How to Break Up with Your Friends*, (Sounds True, January 18, 2022) Chapter 9, Kindle

However you choose to end a relationship, please know that you do not need to stay in a friendship that is destructive or abusive. Your relationship with this person is optional. You have the power to choose your friends. But what about those relationships we did not choose? Family: The people we are entangled with before we are even born. How do we handle conflict within our families?

Family Ties

Ah, family. I don't know anyone who doesn't have some familial relationship that they would describe as complicated. David and I have been blessed with good families with a long Christian heritage, but every moment spent with family isn't conflict-free. Guess what? Families are made up of people, and say it with me, "People are messy!" Good job!

A few years ago, I had an epiphany. As often happens for me, this profound a-ha moment happened while driving. I tend to solve many problems either in the bathtub or while driving. I was driving along and halfway listening to a radio station. It was around the holidays, and a therapist was doing a quick spot on a radio station talking about spending time with families for the upcoming holidays. I hadn't really been focused on the program. I may have been switching channels when the sound from my car radio made me listen and turn up the volume. Something about the woman's voice caught my attention. She had a particularly calming, measured speech with a little Southern twang. Her low, contralto voice melted over me like butter. Listening to her was like sharing a favorite cup of coffee with the kindest grandmother, hugging you as you told her all your problems. I do not remember the lady's name, but if I were to hear her voice, I would know it instantly. In her warm, slow cadence, this is exactly what I heard her say, "Just because she is your mother-in-law does not mean that you have to like her." Wait. What? Say that again. She explained that just because we marry into a family does not mean we will instantly feel a loving connection. She was talking about our unrealistic expectations over the holidays with our in-laws. She continued to explain that a mother-in-law is your husband's mother and will, therefore, be included in some areas of your life, but that does not mean you have to like her. I want to stop and be clear that I am not making any comment about my own mother-in-law. She is a kind woman who has welcomed me into her family. The message I received that day expanded to all my relationships. What the gentle voice said to me that day brought relief in that simply because someone is related to me, through marriage or birth, does not mean that I am going to have a close relationship with them.

As a young bride, I married David. He was my chosen one. The one I would live with until death do us part. I think I had met his family maybe twice before we were engaged. I remember the awkwardness of being instructed to call his parents, Mom and Dad. I didn't even know these people and was to call them by this intimate name?! Not only that, but it felt like I was being thrust into the middle of a story where all the characters knew each other, and I had missed the whole first half of the book. I felt there was an expectation to fall in love with his whole clan immediately.

When you think about it, we did not choose our birth family either. We enter our family story with so much of our history already written. So much backstory shapes our lives as children and carries over into adulthood. I was raised to believe that you were loyal to your family. I was told that family would be there for me when no one else would. In my case, I have found this to be true, but I know many do not have close relationships with various members of their family. Just because someone is related to you does not mean you are going to like them.

> The number of Americans who are completely estranged from a sibling is relatively small—probably less than 5 percent, says Karl Pillemer, a Cornell University professor. Yet only 26 percent of 18- to 65-year-olds in an Oakland University survey reported having a highly supportive sibling relationship; 19 percent had an

apathetic relationship, and 16 percent had a hostile one....Completely cutting off a sibling, regardless of how much it may be deserved, has serious ramifications, Safer says. Those who initiate family estrangement often feel deep regret later. "We have our parents for 30 to 50 years, but we have siblings for 50 to 80 years," she says. "This is the only person who remembers your childhood, and you have nothing to say to them? It's tragic." All the people interviewed for this story say they would reconcile—if their siblings apologized and were willing to start fresh.[85]

Family members can easily push our buttons because they know us so well. As adults, when we go home, we often revert back to our 10-year-old child emotionally. Your family sees you as that same person who grew up in their home. Family relationships can be difficult. The above-mentioned tactics for dealing with heated discussions or debates with platonic relationships can also apply to families. The checklist for unhealthy friendships can apply to family members as well. Here, too, you may decide that some topics are off-limits, and you will not engage in those conversations. Boundaries can be extremely helpful with family members. You may need to set a boundary so no one can just pop in or over to your house anytime. You may have to literally say, "Please call before coming over." Or you may actually need to set up certain days of the week when someone can call you. I knew a grown woman who decided she could never be alone with her mother. Her mom was nice when others were around, but her words became harsh when it was just the two of them. She didn't want to sever the relationship, so with her therapist's help, she ensured she always had someone in the room

---

[85] Sara Eckel, "Why Do Adult Siblings Stop Speaking? The Psychology Behind Family Estrangement and Sibling Rivalries," *Readers Digest: A Trusted Friend in a Complicated World*, (May 12, 2023) https://www.rd.com/article/adult-sibling-estrangement/

when she visited her mom. The only time she was alone with her mom was when her mom was dying. The woman had pushed everyone else away with her sharp tongue, but her daughter stayed. The daughter had expressed how thankful she was that God gave her the strength and soft heart to care for her mom up until the very end. The mother was able to express her gratitude, and in her clumsy way, she also expressed her love for her daughter. It didn't erase the years of heartbreak and struggle, but the daughter was able to extend forgiveness and had some sort of resolution.

Family members can feel they have an inherent pass to mess with your life. The biological connection grants them the right to correct you when you stray from the path they had mapped out for you when you were born. The need to fix family members can be strong, especially when someone feels you are straying from God and entering the realm of sinful behavior. Sitting in the company of people who know you well is extremely uncomfortable when you know they disapprove of your life decisions. It is also stress-producing when you are concerned about someone in your family because they are making decisions you disagree with. When the desire to "fix" someone is strong, it is because you care. And let's be honest, we can feel a lot is at stake. We can feel it as our responsibility to save our families from eternal damnation! No one is responsible for your relationship with God but you. You are not responsible for anyone else's salvation. Love them as best you can and let God work on their heart.

I know several adults who have parents who push their beliefs onto them. The crazy thing is that all these adults' salvation is secure. They know Jesus. They are believers. They are great, good people making their way through life as best they can, but they differ in some biblical interpretations from the ones their parents adhere to. Every interaction with their parents is spent either overtly or covertly trying to sway their kids to "come back to the fold." Instead of simply loving their kids and enjoying their precious limited time together, the relationships are strained and awkward.

When determining if your family situation is critical enough that you want to break all ties, I suggest talking to someone trained in family counseling and conflict to help you navigate this decision. When we sever relationships within our family, the ripple effect will be felt by others. It is inevitable. How will the end of one relationship affect the rest of the family? Fast forward to weddings and funerals. How will these future events play out? Will you attend? Will you be able to remain in contact with other family members?

You should never have to deal with physical, emotional, verbal, or mental abuse. No one should try to manipulate you to do something against your will. Even family must enter your garden through your prescribed gate. They do not have the right to come in and start digging up your life and planting and inserting their ideas at will. Nor do you have complete access to their lives. It works both ways! If your interaction with family is more negative than positive or creates anxiety and stress, love yourself enough to get the help of a professional.

Conflict with God

In the first chapter, I defined conflict as a struggle between two or more opposing forces. Anything that stands between what you feel you want or need creates conflict. Does God ever stand between you and what you want? He certainly has been an obstacle to me getting my way more than once! Are you uncomfortable with the thought of conflicting with God? Does it sound wrong for our will to clash with God's? Should we stuff these thoughts, feelings, and frustrations down deep so that God doesn't know we have struggles and doubts? How lame is that? God KNOWS better than anyone. Should we hide our conflictual feelings from others so that they don't see how weak our faith is?

What about Sarah, Moses, Elijah, Jacob, Job, and David? Sarah laughed at God's crazy plan to have a child in her old age. Even though God had promised Abraham heirs, she stopped believing God would come through with His promise and took matters into her own hands.

It did not turn out well. Moses thought God had chosen the wrong man, himself, to save His people and didn't hesitate to tell God so. Depleted, alone, and scared, Elijah hides in a cave and laments to God that God's plan has unfairly put him in danger and that things are not going well, not going well at all. I picture Elijah slumped on a rock, crying softly, "I've given everything I have to God, and here I am all alone. All alone! No one cares. Not one blasted soul." Jacob actually physically wrestles with God for a whole night over the birthright that God has promised to give him. He's fighting God for something that he wants and that God wants to give him, but Jacob isn't getting what he wants in the way he wants and on his time frame. He is questioning God to the point that there is an actual physical battle. The fight leaves Jacob crippled for the rest of his life. Chapter 24 of Job has a long list of Job's grievances with God, and the Psalms are full of David questioning and, may I even say, criticizing God. Do you sometimes question God? Do you sometimes struggle to understand how circumstances can work together for good? Take heart, friend. You are in good company. It is not the conflict that is concerning. It is our approach to the conflict that is important. Just like you can't control other people, you can't control God either. Woah. Sorry. Is that news to you? Also, you can't hide your doubts, judgments, or emotions from God, so you may as well come clean with him. Tell Him. Have an honest debate with Him. He can handle it. I promise.

It is not wrong to question or even wrestle with God. So much in this unfathomably difficult life could and should drive you to your knees. If you think life is all rainbows and unicorns, you need to look outside of your delusional bubble. There is a big, hurting world out there.

There are parents with special needs children who are giving every ounce of time, energy, and resources to care for their child. For some, they cannot leave the child alone and will never go on a vacation as a family again. For the rest of their lives, they will live with an adult who will never operate above the mental level of a 5-year-old, may never walk, or be institutionalized for life. And what of the child who knows he or she is not like everyone else? He knows he will never be able to care for himself. She knows she doesn't look like everyone else, no matter how much make-up she wears. How could the great Creator and Healer allow this to happen?

What about natural disasters? God can stop storms. He has the power. We know that He can do it. Why doesn't He? Why do the bad guys seem to flourish? Why does evil seem to thrive while the saints suffer? Why will God not answer that prayer you have prayed so many times? Why won't God release you from the pain you are experiencing? There is so much we will never understand. We will never know why. Why does God let these things happen?

In a sermon entitled "Jesus and Whips," Tim Keller points out that in John chapter two, the author has put the miracle of Jesus changing water to wine and Jesus cleansing the temple in the same chapter. What strange events to put right next to each other? Keller unpacks what he believes to be the similarities of these two stories.

> In the wedding feast, you have Jesus acting quietly, hidden, privately. Here in the cleansing of the temple, you have him public and dramatic. There, he was requested. He was asked in. Here, he goes where no one has asked him to go. He intrudes. He intervenes. At the wedding, he brings joy and laughter. Here, he brings weeping and gnashing of teeth.
>
> If Jesus Christ comes into your life, he will sometimes fill your table with a feast and other times, he will turn your table over and spill everything on the ground. These passages show us the authority of who he is, they show us the purpose of what he does, and then they show us the glory of what he brings.[86]

---

[86] This sermon was preached by Dr. Timothy Keller at Redeemer Presbyterian Church on November 24, 1996. Series: The Real Jesus Part 2; His Life. Scripture: John 2:12-25.

God is God, and we are not. At times, I think this is amazingly good news. I am so glad I am not God and that He alone sits on the throne. And then there are other times when I am afraid and unsure of what the future looks like. I can be consumed with doubt and worry. I want to control what happens. I want to keep myself and everyone I know safe.

On February 3, 2021, my beautiful granddaughter, Catherine, was born. She was tiny. When we reflect on the first few days of her life, we can see that all was not right with her from the beginning. Her start to life was hard and complicated. Within her first couple of nights home, she experienced something called "periodic breathing," where she would stop breathing for up to 30 seconds at a time. Luckily, my daughter noticed this and took her to her pediatrician. Her temperature was 91.7 degrees. Catherine was rushed to the ER. Over the next several hours (then days and then months), doctors from 22 different specialties worked around the clock to understand what was wrong with her. Her labs were taken multiple times a day and revealed that many of her organs were failing, most notably her liver. She was close to cirrhosis (essentially, the tissue of her liver was dying). Her incredible physicians eventually discovered that all of this had been caused by a rare reaction to a virus she contracted in utero. After coding and almost not pulling through the night for the second time, she was emergently life-flighted to Houston, Texas (three hours away) once she was stable enough for the re-location. There, another team of highly specialized doctors decided she'd need a liver transplant urgently to have a chance to survive. The average age of a patient requiring a liver transplant is 70. Catherine weighed less than 6 pounds at this time and would be the youngest child ever to undergo this procedure.

Catherine had two brothers, ages four and two, who needed their mom and dad as much as Catherine. Overnight, I decided to go with them and find a house to rent in Houston. We were in this for the long haul. And so, we began the months-long process of waiting for a liver, and this is when my fight with God began. People were praying a liver would become available so that Catherine could have a chance of living a long, somewhat normal life; however, for a liver to be made available for precious Catherine, another baby had to die. I could not understand why God would allow Cat to be so sick, but I really couldn't understand why He would let one baby die so another could live. At this time, my dad's health took a bad turn, and we knew he was near the end of his life. At one point, I wasn't sure whose deathbed I would be sitting at. I lived the circle of life many times in a few weeks.

All of this felt like a curse. Her liver was so damaged, but it ended up being a saving grace that the organ that was damaged most was the liver because a liver can regenerate. Her liver slowly began healing itself from the inside out with its few remaining healthy cells. After 88 long days in the hospital, she shocked everyone and was able to return home to a relatively normal life.

We were so thankful to be home. We were so glad not to have to live in hospital rooms. But why was my heart so heavy? I felt like I should be shouting and singing God's praise for this miracle baby, but my heart was heavy for all those who didn't get the miracle. The many that won't ever get a miracle this side of heaven. All those we saw coming in and out of hospitals designated for children. Why her? Why us? I did not have peace. I had doubts about God's sovereignty. I was more angry than joyful. I pretended to be happy around most, knowing that my feelings were not what people expected nor what I felt was acceptable. I had no right to be sad. My baby had been healed.

Instead of praising and thanking God, I railed on Him. I wrestled with God. I mean, I went after Him with everything I had. I am so sorry to all who did not get the answer your heart has needed and longed for. I will never understand why some are healed and others are not. The foundation of my faith was cracked wide open, and I almost fell through the widening fissure, but God would not let me fall. He would not let me go. He stayed through my rants and my tears. At some point, I stopped looking down at the abyss below me and timidly began to look up. He turned over my tables without so much as an explanation, but He was there for the cleanup. Slowly, the tables were turned right side up, and He laid a feast for me and sat with me as I began again to eat of His bounty. Joy does come in the morning.

Catherine continued to heal; today, she is the cutest, smartest, and sassiest two-year-old we could have ever hoped for. I did get to the point that I could hold her and praise God and, at the same moment, cry for those He did not heal. With tears rolling down my face, I now lift my arms in praise to God, feeling joy along with other conflicting emotions. Both things are true: He is good, and life is unimaginably hard. He is God. And I am not. He is God. And we are not.

In Psalm 22, David goes after God. I mean, he does not hold back. In The Message Bible, the first few verses say: "God, God…my God! Why did you dump me miles from nowhere?

Doubled up with pain, I call to God all the day long. No answer. Nothing.…Are you indifferent, above it all, leaning back on the cushions of Israel's praise?" And, then, he ends the chapter with, "…As the word is passed along from parent to child. Babies not yet conceived will hear the good news—that God does what he says." We will never understand all that He is or why things happen as they do. It is a mystery. One thing I know is that I do not want to navigate this difficult life without Him.

Conflict with Friends, Family, and God

The Mystery

As I come to the foot of the cross,
Eyes downcast, standing at a pivotal crossroad.

Do I follow this Jesus all the way to the end?
Or turn and head in a direction I do not know?

Stories heard as a child of miracles long ago and
Remembrances of fervent sermons and loud amens

Ricochet through my skull and dart to and fro.
Faces of the faithful parade past my closed lids.

I know the old Book quite well by now.
My own hands have turned the pages and worn the cover.

Many scriptures are known by heart. Care to hear a few?
Too many times have I found the verse to prove my point.

And yet, now I stand skeptical at the foot of the cross.
Doubts engulf me as questions bombard my thinking.

The Good Book has become an obstacle of sorts:
Strange rules, murders, relationships, and seeming contradictions.

The Word which has been my salvation and my sword
Now pierces my heart and slices my very soul.

Oh, to have stopped at John 3:16! Why did I read further?
I wrestle with doubt as strongly as Jacob did his angel.

As I come to the cross, eyes downcast,

There is No Bear. Just Breathe.

Afraid to look up and see stained-free boards.

Am I crazy? Has it all been a lie?
My hope for something bigger than me–gone?

I turn and look at the long, bumpy, windy road.
It is a hard road to take. I've walked it before.

To turn away and take the other path seems lonely, empty,
Somehow incomplete. I would miss Him so.

Eyes downcast, distracted by my half-polished toes,
I'm startled to see His dusty scarred feet in front of mine.

He has once again met me where I am.
Embracing the mystery and all I do not know.
I take his beautiful nail scarred hand
And together, we step forward
Once again.

-Kristy Easley

Reflection/Discussion Questions:

- Have you ever had topics you did not discuss with a friend(s)? Was this a spoken or unspoken boundary?
- Have you intentionally ended a platonic relationship? If yes, was the situation handled well? Are there things you would do differently?
- Have you had someone end a relationship with you? What was the understory of the situation? Was there a good resolution and closure to the relationship? What did you learn from the experience?

- Do you think there is a difference between ending family relationships and friendships?
- Have you had to break a relationship with a family member? Do you have boundaries with family members? Do you need to create some boundaries?
- Do you know someone who left God because of life circumstances? Have you experienced moments of doubt due to life circumstances? Have you been able to reconcile with God over those circumstances? Are there areas in which you still struggle to accept God's sovereignty?
- How do you feel about the idea of conflicting with God? If you feel uncomfortable with "wrestling" with God, why do you think that is?
- Have you ever been angry at God's plan and then later seen how everything worked out for the best?

Conclusion

In essentials unity; in non-essentials, liberty; in all things, charity. -Philip Melanchthon

I HAVE SOMETHING to tell you. I did not vote for the same president as you. Now the cat is out of the bag. Phew! That is a weight off of my chest. I just felt like there was something between us that needed to be spoken. And, now that I'm being completely honest, I have some pretty strong negative opinions and feelings about the other guy. Do you feel differently about me? Are we no longer friends? Have you lost respect for me as a person? I am the same person I was a page ago.

There is a 50/50 chance that we really didn't vote for the same person in the 2016 election or the 2020 election. And it's looking like there is a good chance half of us will find ourselves once again at odds with the other half in 2024. Is it possible that we could sit down over cup of coffee and talk about why you voted for your candidate? You don't like coffee? Well, that's okay I know of this really great place that serves all kinds of hot tea. Or maybe we could get a sandwich together? I just want to talk about it, have an honest and open conversation.

I am really not out to change your mind. There is no agenda. I'd love to hear your story and how you arrived at your decision. I would imagine like me, your decision is based on many different ideas and beliefs. I can respect that. Maybe you are still a little conflicted about your choice. I get that. I want to hear all about it. And, if you have time, maybe I could share my thoughts and story as well. I don't know where the conversation will lead, again, I am not out to change your mind. Truly. And, I am not expecting to change my mind but maybe… we could move a few rocks around and learn some new things. What do you say? Can we do that? I hope so. I sure do hope so.

Printed in the USA
CPSIA information can be obtained
at www.ICGtesting.com
CBHW050725130724
11522CB00003B/3